D0327209

...gage your tea

PATTERN *for* EXCELLENCE

PATTERN *for* EXCELLENCE

Engage Your Team to WOW More Customers

Brigham Dickinson

Made for Success
PUBLISHING

Published in the United States by Made for Success Publishing,
an imprint of Made for Success, Inc. Seattle, Washington
P.O. Box 1775
Issaquah, WA 98027
www.madeforsuccesspublishing.com

First Edition: October 2017

Library of Congress Cataloging-in-Publication Data
Dickinson, Brigham
Pattern for Excellence: Engage Your Team to WOW More Customers /
Brigham Dickinson.

ISBN: 9781613398845
LSSN: 2016914788

Printed in the United States of American

DEDICATION

I dedicate this book to my family. May its contents inspire you to live intentionally in the service of your God, your family, friends and fellow men. I am forever grateful for your love, continued support and belief in me. I love you with all my heart.

CONTENTS

FOREWORD
BY MARK MATTESON

I met Brigham a few years ago at Comfortech. What impressed me about him was his energy, positive attitude and smile. This was a young man in a hurry, with a bright future. I told him as much. Over the next few years, I had the good fortune to spend time with him at various events where we were both speaking. My perception and opinion of him only improved with time. It was clear to me he was a serious student. He has stayed in touch and it has been a joy to watch him blossom as a businessman. He has integrity. He practices what he preaches. And guess, what? He is a nice guy.

Nice guys finish first!

His book is fantastic! I read it in two sittings. As a writer of "Bathroom Books" (they are books you can read in four sittings if you don't mind your legs going numb; you know, your "Porcelain Library!") I am enamored of books that come in right around 100 pages. What makes Brigham's book special is it's rich and substantive, filled with great stories, illustrations, insights and process. If you would like to improve the service your company provides, buy copies for all your employees. Make it your "Book of the Month."

The purpose of business is to GET and KEEP customers. This book will help you KEEP more of the business you have.

I'm a little jealous that his first book is so good. Nine people read my first one, no wait, ten, my mother. This book is going to change the way people and companies deliver WOW service.

I have a hunch this is the first of many "Best Selling Books" Brigham will write. Hats off to you my friend. The best is yet to come!

Mark Matteson - International Speaker and author of the International Best Seller *Freedom from Fear.*

mark.enjoythejourney.matteson@gmail.com
www.sparkingsuccess.net

PREFACE
What Keeps Us from WOW?

We forget Why and die from 'Mad How' disease

Modern technology enables us to spread information quickly and more efficiently than ever, but it offers limited face-to-face interpersonal interaction and can rob us of the social skills necessary to interpret our employees' and customers' attitudes or emotional needs. An inability to build these key relationships keeps us from providing great service to others and build long-term relationships.

How I Came to This Conviction

When my son was 18 months old, he was diagnosed with autism. More than 200,000 people are diagnosed with autism in the U.S. each year. Autism is a developmental disorder that is characterized, in varying degrees, by difficulties in social interaction in both verbal and nonverbal communication.

As I learned more about how autism affects the brain and how it is manifested in behavior, I began to notice similar behaviors all around me. Although not autism, I see an ever-increasing number of people who lack the social skills necessary to interpret their peers' attitudes or emotional needs. Whether because of upbringing, personality, technology, etc…there is an inability to create connections, engage in meaningful interpersonal interaction and build relationships of trust.

A second doctor's visit confirmed that life would change with our boy's diagnosis. Days later, we found ourselves at a place called Autism Journeys. The lady reassured us that because we caught it early, we could teach our son the skills necessary to navigate life successfully. He needed ABA (Applied Behavioral Analysis) and speech therapy—all for the low price of $3,500 a month.

What Does Not Kill Us Makes Us Stronger

Neizcthe stated, "That which does not kill us, makes us stronger," which I feel holds an essential truth. I was unemployed when we learned about what our son had and needed. Realizing that there wasn't a local job that could pay enough to cover the continual expense of therapy, I gathered the courage to follow my passion and start a coaching company centered on WOW Experience Training. My wife began hosting charitable events to raise money for families with children who have autism. Both of us found ourselves doing work we truly believed in and felt was greater than ourselves, and as a result we each found more success and fulfillment than we had at any other time in our lives. Out of necessity, we both came to our *Why*.

My Story: Recession Before Progression

When the economy was at a low point in 2008, I found myself five months into a failed business merger. As much as I wanted to blame the tough economy for my circumstances, the truth is that the economy had little to do with it. We were paying our employees to keep the doors open, but there was no money left to pay me or any of the founding partners. Company morale could not have been lower. Fingers of blame pointed in every direction. Eventually, I realized that I could only point to and blame myself.

I had taken a risk that was not paying off. I had moved my family across the country to Florida, away from our home, family, friends, and merged my company with another, becoming a partner in a new business venture. My high hopes for the new venture began to unravel almost as soon as we arrived. Immediately I noticed that the managing partner had an extremely negative attitude. He claimed that he was a realist, but that was just a veneer to justify his negativity. He looked at life with cynicism and pessimism, and his attitude affected us in a profoundly negative way. I felt trapped.

And it wasn't just the money—I had been without money before—it was that I felt obligated to continue on this path and see it through. I had never been a quitter before, and I wasn't about to start now. I felt that I had no choice but to push through, fail or not.

I had lost my passion for the work I was doing, it just wasn't fun anymore. Productivity is hard without the drive to go out and make things happen. My emotional state made it difficult to stay motivated and engaged. My confidence was shaken.

I found myself in survival mode, just going through the motions. I approached work as if it was a set of obligations. I had no energy left, and even "digging deep" did not produce the results I needed. I gave up my freedom and stifled my creativity for a merger that was failing. In my mind, my worst fears became reality.

The environment became so toxic that only with extreme effort could I motivate myself to get out of bed and go to work each morning. The situation deteriorated so badly that I pleaded with my wife not to make me go to work. Not that she had ever forced me to do anything but, in this case, I felt that I needed her permission to stop working. She understood and told me she trusted my decision, whatever it may be. I left for work that morning but couldn't bring myself to pull into the parking lot of our office building —I just kept driving.

If you had seen me driving that day, you would've seen a man talking to himself. I gave voice to my frustration. I placed blame on my extremely negative business partner and blamed the business venture itself. After all, wasn't it the merger of our companies that took my family across the country? Why shouldn't I blame the company for failing five months into our move? My hopes for success were fading quickly, my sense of optimism was lost, and deep down I knew that it was not anyone's fault but my own.

Prayer Answered by a Book

As I drove around that day, through fear and desperation, I prayed aloud, "Dear God, please get me out of this mess." Not noticing where I was driving, I found myself at a bookstore at the far end of the city. As though guided by an unseen force, I went straight to the business section. A book by Jeffrey Gitomer caught my eye. It was a book about motivation and positivity. I bought the book and an audio copy. Imagine it: Starved for positivity, unable to produce it from within, I resorted to an audio book about it just so that I could go to work. Walking to the cash register, I realized I didn't even have the $49.95 to pay for the book, but I knew I needed it, so I put it on a credit card.

Sitting in my car, I played the disc while I flipped through the book. I listened for about a minute before I simply had to turn it off. It was the corniest thing I'd ever heard. I hated it. I couldn't stand the author or the "crap" he was spewing. It took me a few minutes to see just how negative I had become. It wasn't the CD; it was me. Reluctantly, I turned the CD back on.

I vividly remember listening to the beginning of the audio where Gitomer offered helpful instructions to those of us who couldn't stand it, *"give the book to someone else, and watch that someone else get rich and happy."* Having not been able to find the quote since, I concluded that I imagined what he said. Whether he said it or not, he had a point, and it was exactly what I needed to hear. *"If I'm so negative that I'm not open to a positive message, then I'm not ready for a change."* But I desperately needed a change, so I continued to listen. I listened, read, and learned.

I feel that the events of that morning were a divine intervention and led me to that book. This "corny" book that I detested at the moment began to resuscitate me from my coma of self-pity and negativity. The author helped me remember to keep the responsibility for my current circumstances where it belonged, with me. As I started to own up to my part in this failure, I took out a pen and began to enumerate what I knew to be true:

- My bad attitude was not my business partner's fault.
- The business was failing, and it was not his fault either.
- This predicament was on me. I was solely responsible.
- I had let myself come to this mental state, so it was up to me to get myself out.

From One Adventure to Another

What did taking responsibility look like? First was the decision as to the first step in changing my situation. I decided to head back to Utah and start fresh with family and friends near. As I was driving alone back to Utah from Florida, I tried to convince myself that I was doing the right thing: "How can I leave my family with friends? Well, I have no choice. The market is too saturated with competition in Florida. And even if I did find work, it wouldn't be sustainable. I simply have to move on. I have a better chance of succeeding in Utah."

I was feeling confident that I would make something work, but I didn't know what. My attitude was positive. I felt a sense of freedom.

After three days of driving, I was in Salt Lake City resting on a cot in my brother in-law's basement, where I would be sleeping for the next few weeks until my wife and kids came. This offered me some time to come up with a plan. I determined when my family arrived they would not be sleeping in this basement on cots.

As I looked around, just a bit of sunshine came through the small windows near the ceiling, giving me the sense of being in jail. The positive feeling and sense of freedom I felt on the drive over quickly dissipated: "What the hell am I doing? I just left my wife and kids in Florida? What kind of plan is this? I don't have a job—no income whatsoever! They will be here in three weeks, and I'm sitting here on a cot! It could be worse, right? I could still be in a failing business in Florida."

Knowing that my family would be arriving soon and sensing I had no time to waste, I began reaching out to friends and former business associates. I tried my best not to sound desperate, even though that is exactly how I felt. I "worked my network" and was able to find a sub-contracting job selling internet advertising services for local SEO companies. The income was inconsistent, but I was able to make ends meet until I figured out a better idea.

Once my family arrived, we stayed for a month at a friend's house and then moved into a small condo. It wasn't our lovely home in Florida, but my wife and I were glad to be out on our own again.

Although a challenging time, we chose to work hard and keep a positive attitude. We had faith that opportunities would present themselves. In time, I found a niche in the call handling training industry. Because of my background in the residential home services industry, I had several contacts and old friends that helped me get my start training call handling teams. The business grew quickly, and I soon was able to hire a staff to help support the workload.

Experience = Learning, if you choose to change

If hindsight is 20/20, I think I have 20/40! My experience taught me that it's not what happens to us, but how we *respond* to what happens to us that makes the difference. Failure is an essential part of success. Henry Ford said, "Failure is the opportunity to begin again more intelligently." Anyone who has ever done anything worthwhile knows that failing is a part of succeeding.

I began to see that I had a choice in how I acted. I realized that negativity was limiting my capacity to do something better and to create something new. The biggest roadblocks standing in my way were mental, not physical or financial. Circumstances are often outside of our control. Events occur whether we choose them or not. However, it is up to us individually, to choose our experience; to decide the outcome we want and respond accordingly.

I chose to work with a powerful belief, that *when your time is devoted to a practice born out of principle, the work becomes greater than you—and you lose track of time.* Your fears diminish. Technique and stamina are enhanced because of your inner drive to do the work. Habitual distractions dissipate. Outside forces and circumstances gradually fade until all that matters is the work itself. All that matters is the progress and success you experience in doing the work. As Chick-fil-A founder Truett Cathy said, "Fall in love with your work, and you'll never have to work a day in your life." Truett always followed up this quote by saying, "If you are not having fun, then you are not doing something right."

So how do we "fall in love with our work?" Easier said than done, right? It boils down to our commitment to a noble cause, mission, and purpose. It is truly believing in WHAT you do and WHY you are doing it. *"I don't know what your destiny will be, but one thing I do know: The only ones among you who will be really happy are those who have sought and found how to serve."* This quote by Albert Schweitzer speaks to the cause that is greater than you. It is the love of purpose, people, your product, your customer and a cause that is greater than yourself that will give you the ability to transform your relationships, career, and life.

INTRODUCTION
My End in Mind

The why, who, what and how of WOW

I want to make my *end in mind* (my aim or overall objective) very clear up front by engaging in some preliminary Q&A:

Why am I driven to write this book? To show you how to recognize the service standard set by your competition, direct or otherwise, and give you the tools and know-how to exceed that standard in your service delivery.

What dramatic shift is taking place? I see a dramatic shift in customer expectations. Today, customers expect more from your

business than simply the systems, parts, products or services you sell. They see that they have choices. They're becoming more educated and more astute and nearly always turn to the internet first for information. Some either have less money or are less willing to part with their money.

What does this shift mean? Your customers are just a click away from learning your hard costs. They can access websites like HomeAdvisor to compare different services. When they Google your name, they instantly see other customer reviews—good, bad, or otherwise. This transparency means you must offer your customers more than what is expected in order to grow your business, and it starts with giving them an experience they can't get anywhere else.

How can I set my company apart? To get out of the price war, you must win with phenomenal customer service. The internet has leveled the playing field for business. It doesn't take anything more than a Google search to find out that there are plenty of companies that offer pretty much the same products and services at the same price as you—or at least, that is their claim.

In a sea of seemingly endless sameness, what are you doing to set your company apart?
How do you separate yourself from your competition? How can you be better in the eyes of your customers? What can you do that is different than the other guys? What will make you distinct and memorable?

The answer to these questions is simple: Learn to consistently provide an unparalleled customer experience.

What I expect of you, the reader or listener? To study and apply the pattern, principles and practices of WOW service performance. This expectation requires you to be more than a reader (a consumer of my ideas); you need to practice and apply the principles until you master the Pattern for Excellence. It is a journey, not a destination.

How have I designed the content of this book? I have structured the pattern, principles and practices of WOW service in a developmental sequence, and then I address how to apply them for consistent WOW performance.

What do I promise to do for you? To teach you and your team how to WOW more customers, to maximize your bottom line and that you will experience more joy and ROI through the Pattern for Excellence process.

SECTION 1

PATTERN,
PRINCIPLES AND
PRACTICE

What we need to know before we open the door

In this first section, I introduce the foundational pattern, principles, and practices that create WOW Experiences for your customers.

"You can have everything in life you want, if you will just help other people get what they want."

—Zig Ziglar

1 The Pattern

Make great service the new normal

I magine this scenario: You're driving down the road, and you see someone parked off to the side. They have a flat tire. Nothing new here, you see this all the time, but for whatever reason, you decide to act this time and pull off to the side of the road just behind the car with the flat. A young woman is pulling the spare tire out of her trunk. You can sense her anxiety and discomfort, so you offer to jump in and help. She seems somewhat embarrassed but grateful for your willingness.

When the work is done, the driver graciously thanks you again as she opens the car door. You bid her good-bye with a little wave of your hand. Her car soon disappears out of sight. You observe how good you feel about what has just transpired, how this act of service makes you feel. You sense that the driver is incredibly grateful for your act of kindness however, by letting you help her, it was as if she was helping you! Providing a service to her made your day! You feel great and even more willing to do it again when the opportunity presents itself.

Pattern for Working Happily Ever After

Have you ever learned a good business strategy from a fairytale? The story of Cinderella offers some excellent advice if you know where to look.

Here's the basic premise: Cinderella's father dies when she is young, and she is forced to live a life of servitude with her jealous stepmother and vain stepsisters. For years they order Cinderella around, working her to exhaustion. During this servitude, Cinderella avoids growing into a bitter, resentful young woman, because her father had taught her to be a loving, caring person; she faces each harrowing day with a smile and chooses to see the good in others.

Meanwhile, the Prince in the story is dealing with his own hardships. The King and Queen are getting older and are anxious for him to find a wife. In fact, they become so concerned that they decide to throw a ball and invite every eligible maiden in the kingdom—and demand that the Prince choose a wife from those in attendance.

The day of the ball arrives, and Cinderella is so busy primping her stepsisters that she is unable to prepare herself adequately. She does, however, have a dress and at the last minute she runs down to accompany her sisters to the ball. Jealous of her beauty (and fearful of the competition) they rip her dress to shreds, assault her verbally and leave her sobbing in the kitchen.

At the ball, the Prince is clearly frustrated by the horde of women throwing themselves at him and yammering on about their various qualities and how they would be so perfect for him. The Prince becomes disenamored with the encounters. All he wants is to connect with someone who actually cares about him. And in walks Cinderella.

Her fairy godmother had shown up, waved her magic wand, turned her rags into a gown and whisked her off to the ball. Cinderella arrives and patiently waits her turn to dance with the Prince. Cinderella is the first to talk about things other than herself. She engages him in conversation about the music and the dance and even asks him about his interests.

Intrigued by Cinderella, the Prince continues dancing with her and talks with her long into the night until the midnight bells signal her abrupt departure. She runs away, leaving the Prince wanting more; the only thing he has left to remember her by is one of her glass slippers.

The Prince so enjoyed his time with Cinderella that he roamed the entire kingdom looking for the girl who fit the glass slipper. Eventually, the Prince finds Cinderella and, as a direct result of her caring towards the prince, they marry and live happily ever after.

So, what's the lesson here? The Prince was forced into a situation he didn't want to be in—much like your customers who regularly call in or come to your storefront. After all, who wants to take time out of their day for a clogged drain or a broken heating system? Herein lies the takeaway from the fairytale. Because of the Prince's situation, the women of the kingdom were positioned so that they could prey on the Prince—he was being forced to fill a need. The more he interacted with the selfish women, the more his need was ignored—and the more frustrated he became. The women were focused on what they had to gain.

Many of your competitors have this same mindset. Face it—you may have this mindset! Your competitors know the people calling them have a need, and they are more focused on what they can gain from the customer instead of how they can meet their customer's need. Are you taking the time to discover your customer's need? Listen to them, ask questions, learn about their situation, show them that you care, and reassure them that you can help.

As for Cinderella, when she had the opportunity to be with the Prince, she focused on him rather than herself or what she could gain. She went out of her way to do something different. Cinderella exceeded the Prince's expectations and outshone her competition. As a result, she was chosen.

Just like the Prince had expectations based on previous experiences, your customers come to you with preconceived notions based on their previous experiences. Your job is to exceed those expectations so that your customers will go so far as to "roam the kingdom" looking for you. Cinderella listened attentively, asked questions and used the time with the Prince to create value. This is the example of how you can and will exceed expectations and increase your customer base.

Pattern for Excellence

The Cinderella scenario sets the stage for what I refer to as the Pattern for Excellence. I created this Pattern seven years ago and dedicated my time and energy to teaching its principles to thousands of people in hundreds of organizations. The Pattern's end goal is to deliver exceptional service consistently by creating a WOW Experience for every customer.

A WOW Experience is that moment when your client recognizes that you went above and beyond. Expressions such as "WOW," are often used by the client to describe how you exceeded their expectation and won the moment. A WOW Experience is the outcome we look to achieve in every client interaction.

The Pattern for Excellence is a framework for learning how to get the most out of what you do—and learning the best behaviors and practices that consistently deliver phenomenal customer experiences.

You and the Client

Creating a WOW Experience involves two general roles: You and the Client. You must see the work you do as meaningful and be self-driven to provide a service that doesn't consider how hard it is, how long it takes, or how much it pays. It is the kind of work you do autonomously.

In a WOW Experience, you freely provide a service the client did not expect. Clients have an expectation of the kind of service they'll experience for their money. They hope to be impressed and to come back to buy more and tell all their friends about it. You notice the client's impression, and it makes you feel good about what just transpired—and that emotion can serve as motivation to recreate WOW Experiences with more clients.

In a WOW Experience, both you and the client are edified and fulfilled. It's as if a seed is planted inside of you and begins to grow and swell and then to yield fruit because of the natural law of reciprocity. In an ideal interaction, both you and the client walk away edified because you gave exemplary service that exceeded their expectations.

The WOW Experience makes customers come back for more. It makes them more tolerant and patient when things periodically don't go as they expected. We are human; mistakes happen. But if you have created a WOW Experience, you have built trust and loyalty. This trust will bring your customers back and make them loyal to your business.

Companies that stand out today are providing outstanding service to their clients. How do companies provide consistently excellent service? They use guiding principles similar to those in the Pattern for Excellence. They attract people by developing a powerful interpersonal connection. They embody a passionate attitude that is electric and contagious. They are confident in their ability to WOW more customers because they rely on their guiding principles and practice them consistently.

They connect with people by listening to them and hearing their expressions and intent. They connect and become present as they show genuine empathy and respect for their customers. By giving first to create WOW Experiences, they build long-term, reciprocal relationships. The work they do is autonomous in that they endeavor to see clearly what is missing, discover the right answers and respond accordingly, no matter how long it takes, how hard it is or how much they are being paid to do it.

They give others what they really want, what we all want—respect, kindness, understanding—not just what they ordered. They create value within the responsibility they are given and set the example for others to pass it forward. The value they create makes them valuable. They experience fulfillment and happiness in their work because of their attitude towards it—that the work is a blessing that they honor and value because the work is bigger than they are.

As the Pattern for Excellence increases your awareness, you more easily empathize and show understanding. You adapt quickly to create WOW Experiences. You come to genuinely care about your customers. As you master the Pattern, its attitudes, principles, and practices will come naturally and authentically.

Let's Get Started

As we embark on this journey together, I will draw on lessons learned from the past and use personal experiences to show the importance of each principle found in the Pattern's framework. I ask that you consider what you know to be true about each principle taught and write it down. Drawing on your own experience as it relates to the stories and examples I share, consider an action plan that will turn what you know and believe into a habit.

By the time you complete this writing exercise, you will have the tools needed to master the Pattern for Excellence. You will become more aware and persuasive in your communication. You will get more done in less time and increase your ability to create WOW Experiences for your customers.

As you implement the Pattern, you will experience more fulfillment in your work. And, as a byproduct, you attract more opportunity to your business, make more money, and become an indispensable part of any organization or within your own business.

Ask yourself: Do you see your work as a set of tasks to be completed, or is there something bigger at play that helps you enjoy the work that you do? If it is the latter, GREAT, but why? If it is not, why not? What steps can you take to transition from seeing your work as an obligation to seeing it as a principle-centered service opportunity? When will you take those steps? How can you create the conditions and culture that give you the opportunity to do your best work? Take a few minutes before you go on to answer those questions. It helps to identify your "Why."

The Pattern for Excellence provides a framework that you can use to find fulfillment and happiness at work. The Pattern for Excellence focuses on the Outcome: Why; the Principles: What; and the Applications: How.

> *"The goal of life is not really space travel, backyard swimming pools, glider planes, entertainment extravaganzas, big, fast cars, or thrill pills. What human beings are really seeking is individual happiness, self-realization."*
> —W. Cleon Skousen, *The 5000 Year Leap*

2 Principles

Focus on eight Master Principles

G reat customer service is all the rage right now! Well-known companies like Zappos, Chick-Fil-A, and Southwest Airlines have experienced incredible growth because they've learned how to deliver phenomenal customer service consistently to their customers in addition to their quality product.

How do they constantly deliver what we now know as the WOW Experience? They master the art of making timely applications of timeless principles. Mandated policies and procedures usually stipulate one acceptable application. In contrast, principles enable you to make endless applications. The Pattern for Excellence is a *principle-based framework* for learning best practices in delivering phenomenal service. While applying these principles, you will experience autonomy within yourself and your organization and create your best practices.

For example, what do you do when a customer approaches you with a bad experience? Notice I didn't ask about *your company* because it is not as much about the company as it is about *you*. It is you the customer is approaching, and from *you,* they expect results. At Zappos, their *purpose* is not to deliver shoes; rather, it is to deliver happiness to their customer. Zappos employees take ownership of a customer's bad experience, independently of whether or not they are personally involved because they emotionally connect with their company's purpose. They have found their *Why,* and it drives them to create WOW Experiences.

What drives you personally to go above and beyond to restore that customer's trust, friendship, and business?

Eight Master Principles

I am often asked three questions: 1) why these eight principles, 2) why this sequence, and 3) how these principles in this sequence constitute a Pattern for Excellence in both sales and customer service.

The Master Principles are listed in a particular sequence around the *Pattern's* end goal. Each principle in the *Pattern* is needed and carries equal weight in creating WOW Experiences.

1. *Be Positive – Powerful Interpersonal Energy*

Is your passion for the work you do electric and contagious? This principle refers to your attitude toward your work, as manifested in your ability to transmit powerful interpersonal energy with a smile or in the way you go about tirelessly creating unique customer experiences over and over again. Passion for your work also shows through in the amazing service you provide. To say that you need to learn to be positive has become cliché, perhaps because most people have it backward. A clear company vision drives individual behavior. A positive attitude toward what you do for a living is the fruit or byproduct of that vision. Your attitude becomes electric and contagious because to you, the "work" is a cause for which you are willing to fight.

2. Be Confident – Prepared to WOW

Are you practiced and prepared in the work that you do? Your attitude towards your work can only go so far without mastering the mechanics behind it. You need to refine the mechanics to the point where your service looks and feels like magic. Continual training and coaching enable you to work effectively with your peers and learn how to create WOW Experiences. How often do you work on the game that you play as opposed to just playing in it? There is a big difference between professional athletes and their fans. Like professional athletes, you must be practiced and well prepared before the game. Be constantly learning and improving skills. Continual preparation and practice will give you confidence. This swagger, in turn, will make it much easier for customers to believe in your company as well as the services you provide and perpetuate the relationship. With practice and preparation, you can hone your interpersonal skills to create WOW Experiences consistently.

3. Listen – Become Present First

Do you connect by listening first, and by remaining present? This means understanding the expression, tone, and intent of others. Active listening is difficult, even for the greatest of salespeople. Thinking about what to say next as you wait for the customer to stop talking is not active listening. You have to get your mind right by minimizing the conversation going on in your head while others are talking. Just ask yourself if you know what I mean—and you'll know what I'm saying. To be present requires that we turn off the chatter in our heads and requires us to be in a highly aware state. Pay attention to your customer's words and phrases as well as the tone and intent behind their words. Be clear on what they want as well as the experience they are looking for when working with you and your company. Rephrase the content you receive in your words to show that you understand, and ask additional questions to make sure you align with what the customer wants. To create value and a

WOW Experience for your customers, you have to understand what is most important to them first. That is what active listening is all about.

4. Care – Respect Individual Worth

Others can connect and become present as you show genuine empathy and respect for their worth. Do you give others the opportunity to connect with you? Do you show them that you care? People need to feel your sincere concern for them and their situation. They don't want to feel unworthy or less than around you. The inability to connect often occurs when you cannot seem to relate. The word *awkward* has become more prevalent because we seldom understand why others speak or act differently than us. Even when we try to show our concern for others, it comes off as superficial or even fake. The word *sorry* is used so often in our communication that it has lost its meaning. There are so many other ways to express real empathy for one another. *Empathy* is the ability to understand and share the feelings of others. You can empathize with a customer and use that to relate to their situation or need. Simple expressions in your tone of voice as you listen shows that you feel what they are describing. Agreeing with them or expressing that you can only imagine how they feel shows great empathy. If what they are feeling is caused by you, you can apologize, take full responsibility and list specific steps you will take to correct the situation. Showing you care goes a long way in rectifying difficult or awkward situations. They are not *awkward* at all when you show respect for an individual's worth.

5. Say "YES" – Give Beyond Expectation

Do you give first, to create WOW Experiences and build long-term relationships? Customers tend to mirror what we say and do in our interactions. When we say *"no,"* they say *"no,"* when we say "Yes," they often say "Yes" in return. Once I was hosted for dinner by a famous chef named Kent Andersen in Provo, Utah. He stated that he always looks for ways to say "*Yes*" when serving customers at his restaurants. He told of a time when a customer noted with sadness that his banana Foster was no longer on the menu. He immediately sent one of his busboys out the back door to the supermarket to get everything he needed so that the customer could have the banana Foster he craved. *"Yes"* is about giving beyond expectation to create WOW Experiences and build long-term relationships. Focus on what you *can* do for the customer as opposed to what you *cannot do* by always saying "Yes!"

6. Ask – Encourage Autonomous Work

Are you accountable to clarify what is missing, learn the right answers and respond accordingly? This principle is about taking ownership of what you do. Scripts and selling systems help you know what to say and what questions to *Ask* and they can be a good starting point in any position. Obviously, it helps to know your playbook. However, there is a big difference between knowing each play and carrying out each play effectively. The principles in the Pattern for Excellence precede the skill set (scripts and selling systems) because it is essential that you first understand, then perfect the skill. In the *Ask* principle, the notion of *autonomous work* comes into play. Your actions must become intentional in nature; your company's purpose must so motivate you that you do not consider how hard the work is, how long it takes or how much you are being compensated to do it. The service you provide must come from the heart. It must be bigger than you—a cause worthy of your effort. Since every customer is different, you need to ask questions to clarify what the customer wants—the desired outcome to their circumstances during each transaction—and respond accordingly. With this autonomous mindset, a disciplined response to a customer's need or want is not just about knowing *what to say or do*; it is about learning *how to say or do it in response to the specific expectation set by the customer*.

When you are empowered to use your judgment to create WOW Experiences for your clients, you will more consistently provide phenomenal customer service and exceed their expectations. You will become proactive in responding to customers' needs and wants. That is the *Ask* principle in action.

7. *Be Valuable – Inspire Conscious Creation*

Do you create value within your area of responsibility and encourage your peers to do the same? Although you may be *a* customer, you are not *your* customer. Treating others the way you want to be treated is a default or reactive way to serve others. It is much more effective to get clear on how others want to be treated and then proactively serve them in that desired way. Creativity, innovation and maybe a little discomfort may be required on your part. When we endeavor to create value for others by providing a service in a unique and innovative way, our energy goes up. We feel good as we go above and beyond to create WOW and help others feel good. These good vibes between the service provider and client are perpetuated.

When you, the service provider, create value for your clients, independent of how hard it is, how long it takes or how much you are being compensated to provide it, you become invaluable to your company. You become valuable, even indispensable. Be creative in the way you serve others, innovative in ways others do not expect, and you'll experience great satisfaction when you hear them say words like, "remarkable," "extraordinary" and "WOW."

8. *Be Grateful – Honor Our Stewardship*

Serving others together in stewardship is a blessing that we honor and value. When you sincerely thank someone, your expression of gratitude towards them means that they made a difference. When people feel they have made a difference, they feel important and become more connected and loyal to the one that expressed gratitude. Recognizing the time, contribution or effort of another requires humility. Seeing that the work you do needs customers, it becomes a stewardship—an opportunity to serve and create WOW Experiences for others. Doing work that fulfills you isn't work at all—it is a cause that you honor and value.

These eight principles in the Pattern for Excellence constitute the behaviors and framework for learning best practices in phenomenal customer service. Mastery of these principles empowers you to achieve at a higher level and makes you more valuable to the company and clients you serve. You become more aware and persuasive in your communication. You get more done in less time and are able to create more WOW Experiences for your clients.

3 Practices

Practice without principle is obligation

A *practice* is how you deliver a product or service: The action steps, applications or procedures that you use to complete the tasks associated with your job. We have become accomplished at doing our jobs and teaching others how to do their jobs *without first* teaching the *Why*, the purpose behind it.

People are proficient at *practicing* their professions. Mail carriers deliver the mail. Car salespeople sell cars. Orthodontists straighten teeth. Telemarketers answer phones. Technicians fix things. Plumbers, teachers, attorneys, and scientists all have a job to do. Day after day, people clock in and clock out to meet their obligations in the practice of their professions.

Obligation: an act or course of action to which a person is morally or legally bound; a duty or commitment. —*Google Free Dictionary*

When we were kids, we rarely understood why we had to do chores. When we asked, the common response from our parents was "because I said so!" Thus, because our parents "said so" became our motivation.

One of my fondest recollections of my Grandpa was his commitment to creating teaching opportunities while he and I worked together. No matter what we were doing, he took the time to explain *why* we were doing it. His explanations made a remarkable difference because it transformed our work from a list of meaningless tasks to a cause with a noble purpose.

Answering the *"why"* in regards to *"what"* you do is critical because it directly impacts the passion and personal drive you bring to your work. Stop looking at your job as an obligation and start answering the reason *"why"* you do what you do and *"what"* motivates you to do it. Otherwise, your ability to perform at a higher level is hindered as well as your ability to motivate others.

Practice Born of Principle is Service

Principles are the *"what"* in your interaction with others. They identify the values or guidelines that motivate the behaviors in your practice. These principles are fundamental truths that serve as the foundation for a system of individual or organizational beliefs. It is out of this set of principles that your practice is transformed from the mere *obligation* to work into a belief that your work is an *opportunity* for service.

Service (v): the action of helping—*Google Free Dictionary*

As you practice putting the Master Principles to work in every aspect of your life and every service opportunity, you become more persuasive in your communication, more secure within yourself, more open, and work better with others. And a bonus, you get more done in less time. The Pattern provides the principles you need to WOW more customers and experience more fulfillment! We are happiest when we are engaged in a cause far bigger than ourselves.

The Pattern's eight Master Principles serve as keys to unlock the door to *infinite applications* or *best practices* of your creation. This Pattern cultivates the behaviors that you must possess to connect with your clients and consistently provide a phenomenal customer experience. It is amazing how your body will respond to a noble cause. The Pattern's purpose is to create WOW Experiences for those you serve. A WOW Experience is the singular outcome you should look to achieve in every customer interaction.

Example of High-Performance Practices

Texas Roadhouse has a fun ambiance, a ton of food for a decent price, and amazing steaks; they also have free peanuts! After a visit to one of their restaurants, I learned to appreciate Texas Roadhouse even more, and my increased appreciation had nothing to do with their food—it came about because of the busboys.

On a date night, my wife and I arrived at Texas Roadhouse and sat down after briefly waiting for a table. While we ate, the servers performed a couple of line dances that, while not my thing, were entertaining to watch. After one of the dances, I heard a clatter and looked to see what had happened. I couldn't help but get distracted from what my wife was saying because I had to turn around to see the commotion. I only caught a glimpse of a white rag heading back to the kitchen.

Thinking the busboys had just performed a short show, I waited for them to emerge from the kitchen. A couple minutes later, two boys approached the table next to my wife and I. With amazing speed and dexterity, they whisked all the cutlery, flatware, plates, glasses, and garbage into their large plastic tubs and wiped down the table with their white rags—all in less than 15 seconds.

Their cleaning skills were impressive, but what happened next made me a lifetime customer. One of the boys wiped the table with a large circle, stuffed his rag into his apron pocket, and then kissed his hand and slapped it on the corner of the table with that odd sense of wild reverence teenagers are so adept at conveying.

He smiled, spread his arms, took a little bow, and disappeared into the kitchen's steamy confines. No one clapped, no one said anything to him, and certainly, no one tipped him for his performance. But that's what it was—a performance.

I've since thought a lot about how a busboy turned an enjoyable night into an **unforgettable learning experience**. What made him put on such a performance? Why not just clean the table and retreat into the kitchen like most busboys?

Because he chose to be different. For most busboys cleaning tables is a job; an obligation they have to complete to receive their paycheck. The performance of this busboy was an act of service. Somewhere he learned that what he was doing—his practice—was of worth, and he took great pride in it.

Practice to Create a New Path

Imagine that you had to walk to and from work every day. One day, on your way to work, you see a shortcut through a field that shaves 15 minutes off and you decide to take it.

On the way home, you take the same path through the field and save time getting home. For the first couple of trips, you may have a hard time following the new path. But after 15 to 20 trips, you see a clearly defined path. After several weeks of walking to and from work using the same path, you can easily follow a well-defined route through the field, even in the dark.

Now, assume you meet the field's owner at the end of one of your walks. He looks back over your path with mild distaste but doesn't forbid you from walking it. What are the chances you'll take a different path the next day? My guess is slim to none. You now know this path, and you're comfortable with it. In fact, unless the owner specifically asks you not to walk the path, you'll probably continue without thinking. Your path has become a habit—part of your behavioral memory that you use with very little brainpower.

Imagine that one day you discover another path that will get you to work faster and more efficiently than the previous one. You try it and find that it works, but habit always pushes you to your previous path. Despite the old habit, you force yourself to continue to use this new path. The owner of the field is pleased that you've made this course correction. Although the field owner felt there had to be a better way, he didn't have the time or wasn't sure how to help you figure it out. Over time, you notice that the old path through the field has grown back and that the new path has become your new habit.

This story illustrates how you form similar paths in your brain and body. When you have a thought or an action that you repeat over time, it becomes your habit, forged into your memory, mind, and muscle. As you learn new things, you're faced with a choice to continue in the old habit or push forward to forge new paths.

Practice makes perfect. When you practice something over and over, you create paths in your brain. When you repeat certain thoughts and behaviors often enough, a strong connection, also known as a neural pathway, is created. Every time you think in a certain way, practice a particular task, or feel a specific emotion, you strengthen the path. It then becomes easier for your brain to travel this pathway.[1] When it comes time to perform what you've practiced, it's a habit; you don't think about it—you just do it.

The great philosopher Aristotle figured this out over 2,000 years ago; he said, "We are what we repeatedly do. Excellence, then, is not an act, but a habit."

Being excellent at creating WOW Experiences when serving others is the same. When regularly practiced, it becomes a habit. Just like it took effort to forge the new path on your way to work, it will take effort to change your thinking pattern to create value for your clients consistently.

As you study each Master Principle, think about different situations that you experience. Whether you're at work or home, practice using them with your clients, co-workers and family members. Remember to write down what you know to be true about these principles as well as personal experiences that relate to what you are learning. Also, write an *action plan* that will help you turn each principle into a habit. I promise, if you write what you are learning in a journal, the time you dedicate to reading this book will become a transformational learning experience, not just another good read. Your communication skills and your responses to others will become WOW habits, and you'll undoubtedly WOW more customers.

SECTION 2

EIGHT
MASTER PRINCIPLES

*The Framework for Learning Best Practices
in Phenomenal Customer Service*

In this section, we will explore in detail the *Master Principles* of WOW service:

1) Be Positive
2) Be Confident
3) Listen
4) Care

5) Say "Yes"
6) Ask
7) Be Valuable
8) Be Grateful

All other principles needed to create WOW service are "packaged" under these eight Master Principles.

 4 Principle 1: Be Positive The Power of Interpersonal Energy

Our passion for the work we collectively do is electric and contagious

Pre-assessment question: Is your passion for the work you do electric, contagious and attractive?

The human body is a vastly complex electrical system. Your brain sends signals to the heart to keep it pumping, to your lungs to take in oxygen and send it into the bloodstream, your eyes send input to the brain that it "decodes" and interprets. The brain is the center of electrical activity in the body. In fact, the brain creates enough energy at any one time to power a 15-20-watt light bulb!

Almost everything on earth has an electrical system. Quartz crystals emit tiny electrical pulses, which are used to power and regulate wristwatches. A potato creates a small amount of voltage that can power a small electrical device using two dissimilar metals and the juice of the potato.[2] We are all connected to our surroundings and each other in fundamental and powerful ways. These interpersonal relationships have a profound impact on your energy.

Many people experience being either "drained of energy" or "filled with energy" by others. We associate this energy with the "vibes" being given off, whether good or bad. Many people, regardless of their belief in energy transfer, can attest to a person or group of people "draining" their energy. The fact of the matter is that humans can absorb and emit electrical current, which can have more of an effect than you may imagine. In some cases, it could change the path of one's day and possibly even one's life.[3]

Team Vibes

You know what it's like when someone comes to work in a great mood and, just through their simple joviality, inspire the entire team to perform better that day!

It's amazing how much our emotions can affect those around us. Most people who get fired lose their jobs because the boss or co-workers are sick and tired of their attitude and behavior. It has very little to do with their skill set.

Your emotions influence people like ripples in the water. You've seen what happens when you drop a stone into calm water. The concentric rings caused by the rock spread out until they reach the shore or disappear, influencing the water all around them; like your emotions influence people around you.

Go to work each day with an attitude that it's going to be a great day. See how your positive attitude can be a tool when speaking with customers. If you are happy and upbeat with them, they'll feel more confident in working with you—and you will WOW more customers. Use that positive and contagious energy when interacting with your co-workers, and it has the same ripple effect. You will feel more confident as you see your influence and can create more WOW Experiences for customers and colleagues.

Why does a positive attitude have such a big impact on your ability to create WOW Experiences? *Positive attitudes precede positive outcomes*. You have the ability to lead your team to win in their value creation.

Practice it. Look for ways and opportunities to share your positive energy with co-workers and customers. Serve customers and your co-workers in unexpected ways without expectation of compensation or recognition. Then, at the end of the day, consider the emotional connections you have created and you'll likely experience a profound sense of joy and fulfillment.

Why Be Positive?

Imagine that you are shopping for a particular new car at the car dealership. You find one and feel that the car is right. In fact, it's the one you have always wanted. The price is right, and the timing is right. The stars are aligned for you this time because everything is perfect, except for one little thing. You can't put your finger on it until the sales guy opens his mouth and then it hits you. It's the person selling the car. Something is off, but you can't pinpoint exactly what. What is that feeling? Well, it may the person's energy. Negative energy, just like positive energy is contagious.

The first principle in the Pattern for Excellence is to *Be Positive*. When you are positive, you give energy to others; whereas, when you are negative, you take it away. Where positive energy gives, negative energy takes. Of course, many outside forces and circumstances can contribute to or undermine your positive energy source. You want to make sure you're actively working to keep your attitude positive so that you constantly give energy to others rather than take it. How often do you work on your energy? What physically are you doing to create positive energy? Take a minute to ask yourself these questions, discover the right answers, and begin on the path to more positive attitudes and actions.

An Example from Home

My wife had just picked up my oldest daughter, Bela, from school. Her day at school had not gone so well, and so she found herself in a negative state when she got in the car. An argument ensued, and my wife resolved to phone me once they returned home.

Without a word, she handed the phone over to my daughter as I answered the call. As I said hello, I quickly realized that Bela was on the other end of the phone and was not her usual self. Something mean had been said about her at school. It had pushed a normally happy girl straight to a place of severe negativity. The effect she had on everyone around her, however, was alarming. I asked her if she realized that her attitude was making everyone else feel negative, that it was sapping their energy: "Bela, do you see how your negative energy is contagious? You are feeling down, and it is making you exhausted. And you're exhausting everyone else around you. Bela, I think you're a Giver. What I have seen from you is that your positive energy makes other people happy, while negative energy sucks the positive energy right out of others."

What is most interesting about this event is that Bela had no idea how her behavior was affecting those around her. Our energy, whether negative or positive, profoundly affects others.

Dispositional Optimism

Dispositional optimism is the general expectation that good, not bad things, will happen. In 1985, two scientists, Michael Scheier and Charles Carver, were seeking to understand the connection between good health and a positive attitude. They created the idea of *dispositional optimism*. They even created a *dispositional optimism scale* in an attempt to measure the degree of positivity.

Today, over 30 years later, more than 3,000 scientific studies have used this scale to connect positivity to good health. *The Power of Positive Thinking* is not junk science. It's proven science, repeated thousands of times and shows that positive thinking or optimism plays an essential role in your physical health, your success, and your quality of life.

As one researcher, Hans Villarica, reports: "We know why optimists do better than pessimists. The answer lies in the differences between the coping strategies they use. Optimists are problem solvers who try to improve the situation. When they are unable to solve the issue; they're also more likely than pessimists to accept that reality and move on. Physically, they're more likely to engage in behaviors that help protect against disease and promote recovery from illness. They're less likely to smoke, drink, and have poor diets, and more likely to exercise, sleep well, and adhere to rehab programs. Pessimists tend to deny, avoid, and distort problems and to dwell on their negative feelings. It's easy to see now why pessimists don't do so well compared to optimists."[4]

Some life lessons come to us easily—others, not so much. In this chapter, we are looking at our reactions to both external and internal stimuli. I'll share some of the positive principles that I used to overcome my darkest moments. And, I'll share some techniques that I have practiced in my journey toward positivity as well as some ideas about how energy can be both given and taken.

Be Electric and Contagious

How would you respond if the people closest to you asked, "What is it about your attitude that is so electric and contagious?" Can you imagine being so powerfully positive that it impacts the disposition of everyone around you?

Consider the happiest person you know. Is their attitude contagious or does it bug you? Socially, would you rather go out to dinner and be with a couple who is constantly bitter towards others or a couple who is happy and enthusiastic about life?

Be careful how you answer; the people with whom you surround yourself help define who you are. Sometimes we tend to limit ourselves when we commit time to the wrong social groups. Some people can become a negative influence and keep us from being our best. Do the people around you help you have a good attitude? On a scale of 1-10, how good? How do you know? Do you know the story about the frog in hot water? If you put a frog in cool water and slowly raise the temperature of the water, the frog doesn't notice and eventually gets boiled. Sometimes we don't realize the effect a situation has on us. Don't be a frog!

I like to think that everyone can have an electric and contagiously positive attitude. Some are born with a greater tendency towards positivity, the rest of us have to work actively at it daily.

Several years ago, when I was new to the world of sales, I was told, "Brigham, you can't sell." Can you believe that? The person didn't know me. He didn't respect my capacity to become an incredible success, to learn powerful tools and create meaningful relationships with customers. In case there was a hint of truth to his assessment, I began to devour every sales book I could find. I wanted to leave absolutely no doubt that he was dead wrong. In the end, my work made me a much better salesman, and a more successful businessman.

If that manager were to read this book, he would probably expect me to thank him for providing me with powerful motivation. That might be true, but it's equally true that I don't appreciate him. If he had chosen to encourage me, I would venture to say it would have had the same impact but without all of the collateral damage to my confidence and self-worth! Everyone needs positive reinforcement. If he had chosen to be positive and to treat me with dignity, I could have seen him as a mentor and not as someone to avoid.

Positive people always assume the best in others first. It is essential to condition ourselves to look at life in a positive light, not just when it is easy but more importantly, when it is difficult. Keeping a positive attitude gives us the ability to help others gain a positive attitude.

Use the Power of Positive Language

Communicating a positive message about your organization is key to creating a WOW Experience and building your brand. But how is this accomplished over the phone when there are no non-verbal cues for customers?

Here are **six simple tips** for using the power of positive language when communicating on the phone.

1. *Use their name.* Using a customer's name is the first way to create a connection. Ask for it early, and include it naturally in the conversation—but don't abuse it. Don't be afraid to ask the customer how to pronounce it and spell it. Your callers will value this personal touch. If you need to, write it down.

2. *Be sincere.* Customers know when you aren't genuine—they can hear it in your words and tone of voice. Start the conversation by identifying yourself, your company and your purpose. Giving customers this basic information and telling them what you'll provide helps to put them at ease right from the start. Sincerity engenders a feeling of authenticity which allows the customer a feeling of freedom to explain their situation and ask questions unhindered.

3. *Answer questions.* Once the tone is set for the conversation, give the caller answers using positive language. Using phrases such as "*I can't do that,*" "*I don't know,*" and "*just a second*" frustrates callers; instead, focus in on how you can help by stating what you *can* do. Answering questions sincerely and positively builds patience, calms angry callers and helps turn them into satisfied customers.

4. *Speak clearly.* If you've spoken on the phone with a Customer Service Representative (CSR), who is mumbling or difficult to understand, you know how frustrating and tense that is. Focus on speaking clearly, using simple words and phrases which make constructive problem solving easier for both parties. Avoid jargon that is complicated and which only people within the company understand.

5. *Project a positive attitude.* Smile when you answer the phone. It will connect you with the caller. Slow down your rate of speech and vary your inflection to communicate your interest. A

natural, enthusiastic, and attentive attitude helps customers feel comfortable. Always be aware of how your rate of speech, pitch and overall tone affects the call.

6. **WOW *the customer*.** Leaving the customer more than satisfied is the best way to create a WOW Experience. Following the Pattern for Excellence enables you to connect with customers, anticipate their needs and WOW them.

Stop Negative Speech and Behavior

There's far more to this sage advice than simply being nice. Being positive is a state of mind that requires action with our body; it requires you to do something physical, not just mental. It is easier to be positive when life is going well, but it's an entirely different matter when life isn't necessarily going your way. At those points, positivity can be hard to find. Negativity, however, seems easier to find and embrace if you do not prepare for its inevitable occurrence.

Consider the last time you had to interact with a glass-half-empty kind of person. "Glass half empty" is probably putting it lightly. What about the last time you spoke to a person who was being so negative that it began to make you feel negative? I'm betting it wasn't very long ago. Why do negative people ruffle our feathers? I find that the ripple effect that comes from one negative attitude can be incredibly damaging to the overall attitude of a larger group. In effect, any person who brings negativity into the office becomes an invisible sales killer.

Humans are a frail bunch, capable of finding ways to put each other down with the intention of lifting ourselves up. However, if you spend a moment thinking about it, you realize it simply does not work that way. It never has. Thus, it becomes your job to stop behaving in this negative manner.

To limit negativity and foster positivity, try doing four things: 1) train yourself to speak highly of others; 2) be honest with them in the most positive light possible; 3) speak about others with kindness;

and 4) consider the potential greatness of each person with whom you interact.

Note that each of these four actions is **proactive**. Being *proactive* is "creating or controlling a situation by causing something to happen rather than responding to it after it has happened" —*Google Free Dictionary*. We foster positivity in ourselves, by proactively being positive, because *positivity* is separate and distinct from *non-negativity*.

My good friend, Mark Matteson, once told me: "Brigham, your future is so bright that it makes my eyes burn." I felt certain that I was one of a select few that received a compliment like that from Mark. Since then, I have heard him say the same many times to others, but at that moment, it had a positive impact. And by the way, it did not diminish the positive impact the words had on me. It, in fact, gave me more appreciation for how Mark has mastered the art of building others up.

In a way, positivity, in the form of flattery, can get you almost anywhere. What Mark said to me certainly made me feel good being around him. It didn't matter whether he was blowing smoke or not. I remember that he was so focused on me that he seemed to hang on my every word. At the time, I thought that he was an absolute genius to pinpoint my future with such accuracy. Mark's electric and contagious attitude is so powerful that he helped me to see the success in my future as a fact—not just a hope or desire. He helped me believe in myself. This example is a powerful demonstration of positivity in action.

Negativity Creates a Vacuum

Negativity can suck the life out of everything just like a vacuum. Why such a strong reaction to negativity? Back in 2008, when I recognized that I was responsible for choosing my experience despite my circumstances, I began to take the steps that would improve my attitude, and allow it to flourish independently of current events.

I recall feeling incredibly forlorn on the inside but determined to create habits in my life that could foster positivity in me as well as those around me. I forced myself to get up early and run. It felt terrible at first, and I wanted to give up. However, I soon realized the benefits, and it felt good to get out in the morning and breathe deeply of the fresh air.

I developed a set of positive invocations and memorized several scriptural passages that I used while running. It helped me steer clear of the anger and sadness. The daily news was upsetting to me, so I chose to turn off the TV and stop reading the morning news. I then had more time to explore my mind. I learned the value of keeping a journal. For me, keeping a journal helps me to settle the angst going on inside my head and assists me in becoming the author of my life's story. I would often catch myself becoming negative, but learned to respond by quickly writing down a list of things and people for whom I am grateful.

I encourage you to think through what triggers negativity in your head. As you write the triggers down, you become present to your state of being. Next, imagine what is possible. Become innovative in how you process events and consciously create ways to work through those events in a positive manner. Engage your heart and not just your head. Johnny Covey has written in more detail about the "Head to Heart" process in his newest book, *5 Habits to Lead from Your Heart.*

Using these practices, the negativity in me began to subside. Good music and funny comedians on Pandora also helped of course, along with the faith that better days were around the corner. I stopped complaining, and forced myself to see, and then appreciate, the good in my life. It wasn't easy. None of this was easy. Fostering positivity in our lives is tough work. But I can promise you, it is worth it.

PRINCIPLE 1: BE POSITIVE

"There is no situation so bad that complaining about it won't make it worse."

—(Church of Jesus Christ of Latter Day Saints)
Elder Jeffery R. Holland

Fake It 'til You Make It

I felt like Rocky Balboa running in Philly—I was determined to "get stronger." When someone would ask how I was doing, I would say, "never better." At first, it was hard for anyone to believe that. How could they? To tell the truth, I was lying through my teeth. But saying that I was "never better" prompted me to be positive—no matter what my circumstances or how bad I thought it was. I could not let negative thinking affect my state of being because thinking and being are interconnected.

My positive response to life, no matter how fake my "never better" response may have been, soon became real. Although I was aware that there were many times when I felt much better and the positive energy that I created energized the people around me. Their response to my words was positive, and their positive energy empowered me. Slowly, I was getting stronger. Despite my tough circumstances, I was getting good at feeling good, on the inside. I became genuinely content with my state of being.

Near the end of his book, *Yes, Attitude,* Jeffrey Gitomer shares his story of trial and self-defeat. His story is similar to mine: He had to start by forcing himself to be happy. As he continued to exert his energy towards his goal, he found himself in a very positive state of mind. Jeff explains that he can't remember the day, or the hour when the realization clicked into place. What mattered to him, and what should matter to all of us, is that he did it! By forcing himself to think, speak and act positively, no matter what life threw at him, he was able to find genuine positivity in his experience. It was while I was listening to Jeff's success story that I first realized that I also had experienced a change in my attitude. I found that I could relate to his paradigm shift. For me, it was an amazing experience.

I've since read several of Gitomer's books more than once. I have also read other self-help and leadership books from brilliant authors such as Stephen R. Covey, Seth Godin, and John C. Maxwell. Also, the biographies of our founding fathers—Ben Franklin, John Adams, and George Washington—helped me to train my mind and focus on habits that could positively impact my circumstances. My attitude no longer depended on outside influences; I was content in my skin, independent of what was going on at work.

Contentment is sometimes hard to come by. Ask yourself: *Am I willing to do what it takes to find the peace and energy that I crave?*

Training for Positivity

In *The Strangest Secret* by Earl Nightingale, he proposes that many wise people disagree on a myriad of different things but that there is one thing on which they all agree; that the key to success and the key to failure is the things we think about. He proposes that we become what we think.

Training my mind (internal thought life) to focus on positive thoughts was very effective in learning to be positive on the outside (my exterior expression). I found that my positive thoughts were leading me to positive actions. My positive actions led me back to more positive thoughts. Back and forth, back and forth. Thoughts created action and action supported thought. As I built positive momentum in my life, I realized that I was most happy when spending time with other positive people. Positive people surround themselves with other positive people. This is an outcome of positivity.

Years later, I've had a lot of practice and time to think it through. The way I like to approach and increase positivity is to commit to the idea of *being a source of powerful interpersonal energy*. As a source of positive energy, I attract others to myself because of my commitment to positive thinking.

Coolest Kid in Your Class

Late in the afternoon on a sunny day in August 2012, I arrived home after a business trip to happy young voices expressing their excitement that I was home. All four of my kids were twelve or younger at the time, so this was before they became teenagers and aliens took over their bodies. Back then, they thought I was the coolest person (besides their mom); and when I spoke, they listened so attentively.

My daughter Fe, who was ten at the time, told me all about her day at school. She's my California girl who loves to dance and sing. She is spunky and comes across a bit wild. A quality in her that often keeps me up at night considering ways to intimidate suitors in the not-so-distant future.

Fe informed me that her best friend was not her friend anymore. When I asked why, she shrugged her shoulders and said, "I just don't like her." I was quite surprised as the two of them had been inseparable for as long as I can remember. As I listened to her plight, I learned that she couldn't quite remember how it all started, only that they'd been talking behind each other's back and saying mean things.

Bela, my oldest child who was twelve at the time, had a similar experience with another girl at school. For an entire year, the two of them exchanged mean looks when passing each other in the halls. The conflict continued until finally one of the girls spoke up. She asked why they were so mean to each other. Both girls looked at each other in silence as neither could remember. My wife and I asked Bela to consider all the time that they could have been enjoying each other's company had they bothered to ask the question sooner.

With that knowledge, I was not about to let the same thing happen to Fe. I resolved to do the same thing that I strive to do at work every day. "Hey Fe, how would you like to be the coolest kid in your class?" She gave me one of her "well duh, dad" looks and waited for my answer.

I asked, "Are you sure you want to know, Fe? This is for real. This is why people pay me big bucks all over the world, and I'm not going to waste my breath unless you're going to listen to what I have to say."

When she assured me that she would listen, I told her the big secret: "Being nice to everyone makes you interesting to other people. This means you never need to speak poorly about anyone or anything ever again."

I'm not sure if I disappointed my sweet daughter with my "big secret." After all, the idea has been around a long time. Disney's feature film, "Bambi," popularized the adage, "If you can't say anything nice, don't say anything at all."

Fe thought for a moment and then said, "Got it, okay. What's the next step to being the coolest kid in my class?" I knew that Fe wasn't really getting it, so I decided to let the first principle stew for a week until it sunk in a bit more.

The other seven principles in the Pattern for Excellence don't matter much if we don't first address positivity in ourselves. We must commit to looking at life positively and treating others like the incredible people they can be. Positive people are content with life, and draw others towards positivity. Are there things holding you back from moving towards being positive? Questions about our self-worth or feelings of inadequacy can wreak havoc on our ability to be positive. As Albert Schweitzer famously said, "Success is not the key to happiness. Happiness is the key to success."

Clean Your Room

As parents, we try to teach our kids lessons that will provide them with the wisdom they need. Remember the mandate, "clean your room." We couldn't go out with our friends until our room was "spotless." Cleaning our rooms didn't seem like wisdom when we were kids, but now that we are older, the wisdom is plain.

Dad tried to make it simple for me: "It's your room, isn't it? Look, if you can't do something as simple as taking care of your room, how do you expect anyone to believe you have the ability to take care of anything else that you are given?"

In a sense, our rooms were a gift. Our parents must have thought we could handle the responsibility. If you didn't clean your room, your parents might be reluctant to give other good gifts to you. Who knows, they might even think about taking your room away if you refuse to take care of it. Maybe they'll make you share a room with your little brother or sister. We all know *that's* not gonna' happen! So, why take care of it? Because it is *your* room. It is *your* responsibility.

Your mind and your body for that matter are like your room. They are a gift that is yours to do with as you choose. You control what goes into both your mind and body. How well are you taking care of them? Are they clean? Are you taking responsibility for the condition of your mind and body?

As a child, you knew that cleaning your room was good for you, but you likely put it off as long as you could. As an adult, is it possible that you are treating your mind and body the way you treated your room as a kid?

If you were a "normal kid," your mom had to nag you to get on with cleaning your space. As good as kids are at tuning out their parents, is it possible that you are tuning out those aspects of your life that would be much easier to address if your mind was focused and organized?

I remember noticing how, once my room was clean and neat, it felt incredibly rewarding. After I had cleaned it, I liked spending time just sitting in my room and enjoying the space. This fact is doubly true with regard to our minds. Once you address the issues that trouble you and create stress in your life, you are more comfortable exploring your thoughts and experiencing your emotions, creating a "clean room" in your mind.

Cleaning my room was always easier to do once I started doing it. In other words, I used to get caught up in how hard it was going to be. I would notice all of the messes; for instance, I knew about all of the laundry and candy wrappers under the bed. I knew I hadn't done a good job the last time I "cleaned" my space, and I was worried that the work was going to be too much. The same applies to the work you must do to nurture positivity and peace in your head. It is more challenging to *start* the work than it is to see it through.

Once a room is clean, it's easier to keep clean. Did you ever notice how some friends never had messy rooms? These friends emptied their wastebaskets, put their clothes in the laundry hamper and kept their shoes in their closets. They never really let their rooms get dirty. I was always jealous of those friends. It took me a while to learn their secret; they performed a few daily tasks, all of them very easy, which kept their spaces neat and tidy.

Did you ever notice that your friend's room was easier to clean than your own? The same is often true about our thoughts. I have had several deeply meaningful friendships in my life. I can tell you that I am always there to listen to my friends, and to help them through the problems and issues that arise in their lives. Those of us who are good friends to others will note that when our friends bring their concerns, we often believe that we can see the causes of those concerns and the origins of the problems. It seems that other peoples' problems are easier to solve than our own.

At the end of the day, it is our responsibility to keep our minds clean. My mind is my responsibility, and your mind is yours. I am responsible for my self-worth, and you are responsible for yours. Don't try to fix others until you look within and fix yourself first.

Light of the Body is the Eye

Your mind is a gift to you, as mine is to me. You control what goes in. One of the tools that assist us in controlling what enters our minds is our eyes. When you expose your eyes to light, it fills your mind. When exposed to darkness, then that is what fills your mind. Keep your mind clean by exposing yourself to uplifting and positive ideas, people, and things. Ask yourself:

- Where do I spend my leisure time?
- Who is in my circle of influence?
- Do they bring light or darkness into my life?

You must learn to embrace the light and avoid darkness that can bring you down. Examples of darkness can include the news, bad friends, smut and dross from media or anything else that can bring you down or allow in the darkness. Drugs and other addictions can keep you from being what you are meant to be. Porn is darkness—a disease to avoid at all costs. Shut these and all other forms of darkness out of your life and let the light and positive energy flow through you. Read from the greatest books. Listen to uplifting music. Subject yourself to light and avoid the dark.

Practice Being Positive

You have the ability to choose the mood you are in, and choose the attitude you embrace. By choosing a positive attitude, you can get out of a bad mood faster and attract people to you. People will want to be around you. Your positive attitude helps them feel better—and be more successful. Abraham Lincoln said, "*Most people are about as happy as they decide to be.*"

How can you train yourself to be positive? Here are *12 tips* you can use to develop a more positive attitude:

1. *Practice being positive*. Because your attitude is your choice, you may need to practice making better choices. Studies show that it only takes 90 days of repeating an action before it becomes a habit. So, in as little as 3 months of making the right choice, your attitude will be better, and you will be a more positive person.

2. *Learn something new*. Engage your mind and celebrate your successes as you progress toward an achievable goal. Maybe you've always wanted to play an instrument, learn a new language, paint, or cook. Whatever it is, find something that you enjoy that will stretch you. You'll find it to be refreshing, and it will give you a more positive attitude.

3. *See the good*. Too often it is easier to recognize the negative aspects of your day than the positive. When you make a concerted effort to focus on the good things, you find that more and more good will come your way. Some people like to keep a journal of good things that happen to them throughout the day. A journal is an excellent way to see the good in your life.

4. *Recognize your value*. Look at the positive things you have achieved in your life and recognize your value and worth. You will be inspired to continue seeing the positive as you understand you are valuable.

5. *Play.* Indulge your inner child and play. Whatever it is you enjoy doing, do it routinely. As you engage in activities you enjoy, endorphins enter in your system and give you more energy.

6. *Associate with positive people*. Simply by being around positive people, you pick up on traits that you can use to stay positive. Notice things they do and say, or don't do and say, that you like and make an effort to emulate them.

7. *Smile and laugh more*. When my kids are in bad moods, I find that if I can get them to crack a smile, their happy demeanor soon returns. Laughter *is* the best medicine. American humorist Bennett Cerf wrote, "*The person who can bring the spirit of laughter into a room is indeed blessed.*" I've learned that laughter

is a key to my positivity. To maintain a positive attitude, I look for opportunities to laugh with my children, wife, and friends.

8. *Greet people with a smile, wave or handshake.* Recently, on my way to work, I noticed an elderly woman walking to get her morning exercise. What impressed me is that she gave a big smile and a wave to each and every person that passed by. It put a huge smile on my face. The next time I saw her, she did it again with the same enthusiasm. She seemed truly genuine in her positive wishes. Once again, she changed my energy level. Now, when I drive to work, I wonder, "Will I see the happy lady today? I could use a dose of positivity!" You don't need to run out and start waving at people, but if you smile and try being more upbeat and maintain a positive outlook, more people will want to work with you and buy from you.

9. *Listen to great comedians* such as Jim Gaffigan or Brian Reagan (avoid rude, crude and obscene comedians). Great comedians make you laugh, and laughing improves your state of being. You can find a plethora of funny and wholesomely entertaining videos on YouTube or Pandora.

10. *Serve and act unselfishly*. The wise words *"I got more out of helping others than I gave"* has its roots in 5,000 years of human discourse. Consider the combined wisdom of Cicero, a Roman poet who lived before Christ, Warren Buffett, the 'Oracle of Omaha,' Albert Einstein, and Will Smith.

> *"Not for ourselves alone are we born."*
>
> —Cicero

> *"If you're in the luckiest one percent of humanity, you owe it to the rest of humanity to think about the other 99 percent."*
>
> —Warren Buffett

"Our task must be to free ourselves... by widening our circles of compassion to embrace all living creatures and the whole of nature in its beauty."

—Albert Einstein

"If you're not making someone else's life better, then you're wasting your time. You will become better by making others' lives better."

—Will Smith

11. ***Take care of yourself physically.*** Sleeping well, eating right and exercising regularly strengthens your body and helps you stay healthy. Recognizing that how you feel physically plays a powerful role in your mood and outlook. This physical component cannot be overstated.

12. ***Consider what you are grateful for and write it in a WOW journal.*** Practice being grateful by writing all that you are grateful for in one minute. You will be able to think of more things for which you are grateful as you practice. Look at writing in your *WOW Journal* like you are writing the script of your life. Journaling enables you to remember your inspirations, create invocations, re-read your thoughts and to reflect upon the wisdom that carries you through your darker moments. When journaling, keep your mind fixed on what is most important to you. Avoid distractions. Set a target and do not rest until that goal is achieved. Reward yourself for both failure and success. Celebrate effort, not just progress. Enjoy the journey as you focus on your destination. Taking the time to write and read a journal is an empowering and uplifting experience. I encourage you to engage your positivity by keeping a journal. It just may be the beginning of an incredible story.

PRINCIPLE 1: BE POSITIVE

These 12 tips will guide you in developing a positive attitude and in succeeding at work and in your relationships. As you cultivate a positive attitude by making time to work on it each day and giving others energy, you'll be better at what you do and much more effective at creating value for others. So, apply those tips that work best for you and create WOW Experiences by being positive.

5 Principle 2: Be Confident Prepare to WOW People

We are practiced and well prepared
in the principles we teach

Pre-assessment: How confident do you feel in the role you play at work?

To boost your confidence, apply this principle: **Preparation bolsters confidence.** The following two stories illustrate this principle.

Who is the best receiver of all time in the NFL? I nominate *Jerry Rice*. Why? It didn't matter what the coach was trying to do during practice, if you threw the ball to Rice, you knew he was going to catch it and run for a touchdown. He was the first one on the field and the last one to leave. He was an incredible talent but also outperformed the competition. He was continually working on his game. Rice once said, "Today I will do what others won't, so tomorrow I can accomplish what others can't." Jerry Rice won games because of the way he prepared. What does your preparation look like before you "play"? Are you a professional? What steps are you taking to improve your ability to perform?

What was the source of Jerry Rice's confidence? He was always working on his game. When he caught the ball in practice, he ran the full distance of the field for a touchdown. Can you imagine? You are practicing on one end of the football field, and as soon as you throw the ball to Jerry, he's running down to the other end of the field to make a touchdown. You might think this was disruptive to everyone else trying to practice, but Jerry knew what he was doing. Receiving. His responsibility was clear. Receivers catch the ball and run it in for a touchdown. He developed his speed by running five miles on hills every morning during the offseason. He recognized that when everything was on the line his performance depended on his preparation. Quarterbacks like Joe Montana and Steve Young sought him out on the field because they saw how hard he worked in practice. Jerry's self-confidence motivated Joe and Steve to believe in him too. They had confidence that he would perform—catch the ball and run it in for a touchdown.

What are you doing to improve your game before playing? How often do you practice before the game starts? If you work in a call center, for example, are your calls tracked and recorded? Have you ever listened to them? How often should you listen to your calls? Do you have a coach who evaluates your progress and gives you pointers on how to improve regularly? A quote attributed to Henry Ford (although some think is what Albert Einstein), "If we do what we always did, we will get what we always got." Preparation and continual practice give you confidence. It is up to us to learn, adapt, change and improve our performance so that we receive the results we desire. As our confidence increases, so does the confidence of those around us.

Can you remember being told that you can do anything you set your mind to? Do you believe it? No question, some are born with innate talent in one field or another that makes it easier for them to achieve their dreams. However, everyone is born with one talent or another, and you want to consider where your strengths lay and what you enjoy doing before choosing a career path. But what if you're not built like Shaq O'Neal? Chris Paul and Steph Curry aren't built like Shaq. They probably had to work harder to play at Shaq's level, but they did it! At the end of the day, everyone has to work hard to achieve at a higher level. It's all about developing a belief in your capacity for improvement and putting in the work to make it a reality.

Since I'm talking about basketball, I'll ask you, "**Who is the greatest basketball player ever?**" Answer with the first response that pops into your head. Perhaps you thought of Wilt Chamberlain, Kareem-Abdul-Jabbar, Pete Maravich, Bill Russell, Koby Bryant or LeBron James? All of these amazing athletes are great options, but my guess is that you first thought of Michael Jordan.

Jordan is widely considered the greatest basketball player to have ever played the game, but he was not always the greatest. In fact, Jordan was cut from his high school varsity team because he was considered too small and not quite good enough to make up for his size.

Most people, when told they're not good enough, let this kind of negativity sink in and they often surrender to mediocrity; Jordan could easily have been one of these people. I'm sure that after getting cut, he had hard days when he considered believing the negative input; but he chose to rise above it instead.

He had a dream, and he used that to motivate himself. He trained, practiced, and prepared to learn the skills needed to achieve his dream. The following year, not only did he make the team, he was a standout player. The rest, as they say, is history, but it all started with Jordan making the decision to do whatever it would take to become a great basketball player. He seized his opportunity and increased his capacity to play— and it turned out pretty good!

How often are we faced with similar situations? How many times have you had a chance to improve, and then capitalized on it? Opportunity surrounds us! The problem we often face is not our capacity to perform; it is a lack of belief and an unwillingness to put in the work necessary to take advantage of those opportunities.

Practice Being Confident

Several years ago, I took a job in Chico, California. I had just completed my bachelor's degree in marketing and was excited about the new adventure. I accepted an offer as the Marketing Manager and Lead Coordinator for a local heating and cooling company. I was responsible for answering in-bound phone calls from potential system replacement customers.

I didn't see much value in the call handling part of my job. Answering phones was not on my career path and, sadly, I felt a sense of superiority to it. Not until my district manager paid me a special visit, did I learn that what I was doing was critical to the success of the company.

My manager's name was Kevin Comerford. He was responsible for the success of several heating and cooling companies on the west coast. A real-life bigwig. I was thrilled that he was coming to Chico to have a sit-down with me. I assumed, of course, that it was because of my marketing genius.

As soon as I was made aware of his visit, I began to prepare some new marketing concepts that would build the company's brand and get the phones ringing. Why else would he want to speak with me, right? Nothing like one's ego to get in the way of rational thought.

When Kevin arrived, I was nervous but confident in my marketing plan for the company. We exchanged pleasantries as he showed me to the meeting room and closed the door. He sat on the opposite end of the table from me. We chatted about my job and how it was going. I cordially answered his questions, waiting for the perfect moment to present my marketing plan.

Soon my opportunity arrived. He asked me how the marketing aspect of my job was going, and I skillfully launched into an elaborate marketing plan monolog. Kevin nodded a couple of times while listening patiently to my torrent of ideas and explanations.

After five minutes of what I believed to be pure marketing brilliance, I finally had to take a breath; Kevin seized the opportunity to ask a question, "That's all great stuff, Brigham, but on a more important note, tell me how you are doing on the phones?"

I reeled, totally thrown off my groove and not knowing quite how to respond. Here I was in the midst of what I thought was going to be a career-defining moment, and Kevin asks me about how I answer the phones! I could feel befuddlement beginning to spread across my face. I blurted out the most profound answer that came to mind, "It's good. It's really good."

Kevin smiled, "Let's practice. Show me how you would handle a customer call."

My first attempt was aweful, and so was my second. Kevin paused to remind me that the expectation of the customer has never been higher and that I needed to do much better to meet and exceed those expectations.

I soon realized that call handling quality was Kevin's true intention for our meeting. The next two and a half hours were indeed career-defining, but not in any way what I had anticipated. With the patience of a monk, Kevin coached me through every customer concern he could think of.

While we worked together, I realized just how much I had to learn and how many opportunities I was losing because I handled the calls incorrectly. My superiority complex around call handling evaporated quickly. The company could lose thousands of dollars in long-term relationships if I did not up my game.

He had me write a call script, and we practiced it, refined it and practiced it some more. He wasn't as concerned about the script as he was the reason behind it. He reminded me that every other position in my company relied on my position. I was their front line.

He would say, "Nothing good can happen until we book the appointment." If the customer didn't like me, there was little chance that they would buy from the company I represented. After a grueling two and half hours, he looked at his watch, thanked me for my time and stood up, signaling the end of our training session.

Turning around just as he was walking out the door, he informed me that he would call in periodically, pretending to be a customer so that he could verify I was still using the script and ideas we had created together. "Even if you recognize my voice," he said, "continue treating me as if I were a real customer." He thanked me again, and slowly closed the door as he left.

As promised, Kevin called in about every two weeks for approximately six months. On some calls, he was a cowboy straight out of a Louie L'amour book. On other calls, a New Yorker with a heavy accent. He was also once a southern gentleman. But my favorite was the time he tried to pull off being an elderly woman; let's just say I had a lot of fun, and it made a lasting impression.

Regardless of which identity he used, Kevin always ended the call by reassuring me it was him, not a real customer. I would feign my surprise and reassure him that I again was fooled. What I appreciated most was that he took the time to provide feedback on how I handled the call.

He always reminded me how important my job was—that I provided the customer's first impression of the company. The concept he impressed upon me was that the customer buys *me* before he buys anything else my company has to offer.

Hence, I learned to appreciate answering the phones. It helped that I was quite good at it too. Within a few months, I was having so much fun that I could have continued with it for years. My customers became my friends; my top priority was making sure they received the help they needed. I began to enjoy taking calls much more than marketing. I was passionate about my phones and it showed. Kevin's training made me well-practiced and prepared. Our incoming phone volume increased to such a degree, we had to hire more people. I attribute this to the confidence I gained with Kevin's coaching. My confidence and success spilled over into my team. I became indispensable as a lead coordinator, thanks to Kevin. I was grateful for the time he dedicated to preparing me to perform at a consistently high level, no matter what customer called our office.

Prepare or Perish

One of the Bible's most famous lessons is contained in Christ's "Parable of the Ten Virgins." In this parable, Christ explains that ten virgins were waiting for the bridegroom to arrive for the wedding feast. Five of the virgins came prepared with oil in their lamps in case the bridegroom came during the night; the other five brought their lamps, but no oil. Sure enough, at midnight the call came that the bridegroom had arrived. The wise virgins, those with oil, began preparing their lamps so they could go out to meet the bridegroom. The foolish virgins, those with no oil, asked the wise virgins to share with them. The wise virgins refused, explaining that there would not be enough oil for everyone and suggested the foolish virgins go out and buy oil for themselves. While the foolish virgins were gone, the bridegroom arrived and welcomed those with their lamps lit to the wedding feast. When the foolish virgins returned, they were refused entrance to the feast because the bridegroom did not recognize them in the dark.

The lesson can come off harsh, but the principle holds true. The foolish virgins missed a great opportunity because they did not adequately prepare. Being shut out had nothing to do with their belief because they clearly believed the bridegroom would come, they just failed to prepare. In addition to the obvious lesson in this parable, an additional lesson to point out is: *Belief is not a sufficient substitute for adequate preparation*. One must prepare to take advantage of the benefits that opportunities offer.

What are some ways you could be better prepared and thus become more confident?

Keep Working at It: 10,000 Hours

In 2008, Malcolm Gladwell published *Outliers*, where he outlines a well-researched map for success. That map discounts talent and IQ for the most part and instead focuses on doing the work and gaining experience in your chosen field.

Gladwell admits that talent, timing, and IQ certainly help; however, according to him, working and gaining experience adequately prepares someone to take advantage of their opportunities. Gladwell points out that gaining this experience is not something done quickly; in fact, he states that the magic number for success is *10,000 hours* of practice.

Gladwell uses Bill Gates and The Beatles in his *Outlier* thesis. Bill Gates was successful largely because he had the good fortune of attending a school that gave him the opportunity to program computers for more than 10,000 hours before he ever started his company Microsoft.

The Beatles, without question, had musical talent, but what enabled them to become a worldwide sensation was an invitation to play in Hamburg, Germany. While in Germany, they performed live, sometimes up to five hours a night, seven days a week. That opportunity to practice allowed them to refine their abilities so they could take advantage of the opportunities they later encountered. It was during this time they found their unique sound.

Are both Bill Gates and the band members of The Beatles talented? Absolutely. But they also put in a lot of hours refining their skill and perfecting their talent. Gladwell's prescription states that practice isn't something you do once you are good; it is the thing you do that makes you good. So practice. Do what it takes and then take advantage of the opportunities your hard work creates.

Assessment: In what areas do you need to put in more time to become the best?

Self-belief is at the core of having **self-confidence**. However, don't mistake arrogance for confidence. Confidence is a feeling of self-assurance arising from your appreciation of your abilities or qualities. On the other hand, arrogance is an exaggerated sense of your abilities or qualities. The word *appreciation* helps separate confidence from arrogance. Appreciation is a full understanding of a situation or gratitude for something. When you are confident, there is no self-delusion. You are certain of your ability, but you're able to keep that certainty in perspective. People are attracted to those with confidence. They're turned off by those who come across as smug or arrogant.

Preparation produces confidence. So, set worthy goals. Do not let yourself become distracted. Put in the work. Work smarter—not just harder. Make time to learn daily and choose to believe that in time, the right doors will open and more importantly, that you will have the capacity to confidently walk through them.

> *"Being busy does not always mean real work. The object of all work is production or accomplishment and to either of these ends, there must be forethought, system, planning, intelligence, and honest purpose, as well as perspiration. Seeming to do, is not doing."*
>
> —Thomas Edison

Grandfather's Wisdom: Work Smarter

As a young boy, I thoroughly enjoyed waking up to the sweet sound of singing birds outside my bedroom window at my grandparent's home in the small town of Kanosh, Utah. My mom would often send me there for the weekend. I can't imagine why, of course, since I was the spitting image of perfection in my youth. In fact, my mother has told me countless times that if I had been her first child, I would also have been her last. Now, don't get me wrong—she is a woman of great faith, having three (normal) children before me and then actually had two more!

My room at my grandparent's sat between a storage room and my grandparent's bedroom. It was quiet, except for the birds, and I would often spend part of the morning lying in bed with my hands tucked up under my head listening. In spite of how much I enjoyed lying there, my restless young body wouldn't allow me to lie still for too long, no matter how sweet their sound.

Succumbing to my boyish energy, I would get up at 6 am and hop onto my grandparents' bed. It was the tradition to lay there for a while and enjoy their company, talking about how we slept or giggling about this or that. When the traditional morning chat came to a close, Grandpa and I would get up and go to get milk from the dairy up the street. I remember how amazing it was to see where milk came from and how the farmers herded all those cows in for milking.

After returning home with the milk, Grandma would have a warm breakfast waiting. After eating, Grandpa and I usually did some work on his land—mowing the lawn, pulling weeds and picking rocks out of the garden.

The thing I appreciated most about my Grandpa was his commitment to creating teaching moments while he and I worked together. Whatever we were doing, he took the time to explain the *why* behind what we were doing. His explanations made a remarkable difference because it transformed our work from a list of tasks to work that felt noble and purposeful.

I remember once when my Grandpa took me out to a pile of rocks behind his shed and asked me to move them about 25 feet away and put them in a new pile. Grandpa was vague in his instruction and I was a little confused and somewhat bothered when he left me to do it by myself.

He asked me to move the rocks and then left me to decide how I was going to do it. Perturbed, I stared at the pile for a good solid minute and then decided to grab a shovel from the shed. One shovel at a time, I moved the rocks from one pile to the next. It was tedious work, and I felt it would never end.

When Grandpa came back to check on me, he quietly watched for a few minutes and then to my surprise, he left. I started to call out to him to see why he acted so weird, but he was already around the corner of the shed and couldn't hear me. I stood there, puzzling over his actions. Grandpa soon came back around the shed pushing a wheelbarrow and wearing a big smile.

"Brigham, work smarter not harder."

Those four words completely changed my perspective. It was much easier loading up the wheelbarrow with rocks and then wheeling them over to the other pile. This tangible example showed me that it made more sense to *work smart*—not hard.

Virtually every day since then, Grandpa's words of wisdom have reminded me to use my head and *work smarter*. In every endeavor, I consider more efficient ways to do what's needed, and it has served me well. Thank you, Grandpa.

Have faith in yourself. Avoid the naysayers, especially those closest to you. When I first started my training company, few believed that I would succeed. Some laughed at the thought that I could go anywhere with my idea to train call handling teams. I persisted, knowing that as long as I kept at it, sooner or later, I would get my shot. It required sacrifice and hard work, but it paid off. Believing in yourself is an essential ingredient to success.

Get on the Right Path and Never Give Up

When I first started my business, if you remember I was sleeping on a cot and working in my brother-in-law's basement. I made innumerable phone calls to friends and associates. I read every sales and self-help book I could get my hands on, listened to CDs, recorded my voice for self-evaluation and wrote my thoughts in a journal.

I was on a mission to find purpose and make a difference in the world! I did not know where I was going exactly or when I would get there. I just knew that if I kept working at it, I would soon experience success.

In the early days of my internet advertising business, I was keenly aware of how important each client was to my success. One of these clients had a knack for keeping me up at night, but I couldn't lose him because he was one of only three accounts! He often expressed concern about his call conversion. Since his call handling team wasn't booking appointments, his sales team were "sitting on their hands." What was the point of internet advertising if they could not convert a potential customer into a buying customer?

I convinced him to record his calls to discover why his team's success rate was so low rather than cancel my service. Within two weeks he called me to announce that he was ready to fire his entire team. I gasped. "Let me train them," I said, confident that I could turn this situation around by helping his staff improve their skills. With some reluctance, he resolved to give me a month.

Inside of three weeks, I successfully retrained a few members of the team. They now focused on creating WOW Experiences for their customers over the phone, making me look like a total superstar. Initially, all I wanted was to save a client from canceling his advertising. But I quickly realized there was far greater potential—I started a new company, training call handling teams to WOW their customers over the phone, book more calls and make more money.

When I told my client that I was starting a new company training call handling teams, he referred me to all of his business friends! I had made that much of an impression. Referrals are the highest form of praise for a business. What I find so funny, is that the job I had taken in Chico, California, that I had initially bumbled, had turned out to be the best training and experience I could have received to prepare me for this new business venture. Pushing through the hard times often trains and prepares us for the future, and most of the time we don't even know it.

Assessment: Are you on the right path and just need to keep pushing on?

Persistence Pays—in Five Dollar Bills
Abraham Lincoln was born February 12th, 1809. Mostly self-educated through avid reading, Lincoln became a Kentucky

politician and an accomplished attorney. He was known for his stark opposition to slavery. He saw it as a sin and contrary to his belief in the equality of all men as expressed in the Declaration of Independence.

Committed to his cause, he ran for a U.S. Senate seat in 1854 and again in 1858. He failed both times even though he was gaining in public popularity. In his second Senate race, he ran against Stephan Douglas, a fiery politician known as "The Little Giant" for his short stature, large head, and broad shoulders. Douglas and Lincoln entered into a fierce debate over slavery. On opposing sides, they produced seven of the most famous political debates in American history. Lincoln won more popular votes. Douglas more seats. Therefore, Douglas was re-elected to the U.S. Senate.

Lincoln's persistence and passion soon rendered fruit. Though Lincoln suffered another bitter defeat in his second Senate race, his articulation on slavery and other issues helped him build a national reputation in politics. And in 1860, the Republican State Convention nominated him to run for President. The Democrats nominated Stephan Douglas to run on the Democratic ticket but with 180 electoral votes Lincoln won; a virtual landslide. Lincoln was persistent and did not give up. He saw that there was a cause, of noble worth, that was greater than himself.

The ideas found in the Declaration of Independence and the U.S. Constitution are not new. Penned by Jefferson, Franklin, Sherman, Adams, and Livingston, the ideals presented in the Declaration are based on the studies and writings of the greatest leaders and philosophers throughout recorded history. Our Founding Fathers put their ideas about a free republic into practice…and the rest is history.

Develop Greater Confidence

When things are not going well, and you feel like it has gone on forever, it can be hard to find the motivation to press on. But when you believe in the purpose behind what you are doing, you can keep moving forward in spite of the adversity. For our Founding Fathers, it was *liberty or death*. Why? Because they did their homework, they knew that what they were doing was right, and it was worth fighting for no matter the cost or how long it took to obtain it.

When you are willing to do the work and believe in the process, amazing things happen. It is not just about the results; it is about who you become in the process. True confidence is something deep inside you. That part of you that believes you can make a difference regardless of external factors.

Can you imagine JJ Watt, arguably the best defender in professional American football, saying he doesn't need to watch films of his games or the games of his opponents anymore? Can you imagine him saying, "I don't need to practice?" Can you imagine him saying "I don't need a coach?" He is a professional, and professionals know better than anyone that practice and preparation wins games.

What are you doing to ensure you win your games? The principles and practices in this book lay a foundation to improve your confidence. It is up to you to build on that foundation. Do the work that builds confidence.

Assessment: Are you a professional? How often do you work on your game?

Do you practice and prepare before your game starts? Are you ready to develop a new level of confidence? Write your answers down in your journal. Consider what you know to be true about this principle as well as experiences you have had that relate. Write an action plan to form habits of continual practice and preparation to improve your game.

6

Principle 3: Listen
Become Present First

We connect by listening first and remain
present to the expression, and intent of others

Pre-assessment question: Are you listening to your customers?

S uppose you work with a residential heating and cooling
company and the customer on the phone is very upset—not
at you, just the situation. It's hot in their home, the A/C's
broken and their mother-in-law is complaining about the heat. They
cannot survive another day without A/C. Their son, who is only four
months old, is crying in the background, and you respond with,
"What's your address?"

Are you listening to what they just said? Are you taking the
time to show them you understand? If they said their house was
on fire, you would not ask, *"Have we done work for you before or
where are you located?"* Engage with the customer by seeking first to
understand and empathize. Then, respond accordingly.

When you meet a customer in their home, you don't want to
barge in like a firefighter ready to put out a fire. Take a minute, show
them that you want to understand their situation. Give them the
opportunity to share their frustration and feel that you empathize.

The customer has an emotional need to be heard and understood.
That's why so many go into detail when they explain their situation.
By rephrasing what they just said and asking additional questions,
you show them you heard them, understand, and are willing to help.
Their disposition begins to change. You will see their demeanor

change when they feel understood. Attentive listening helps the two of you connect, and creates a bond of trust. When they trust you, the rest is easy.

Assessment: Do you connect by listening first and remaining present to the expression, tone, and intent of others?

Even some of the best service reps and salespeople struggle with their listening skills. Once you start talking, it is hard to stop. People have a need to be heard and understood. You cannot connect well with others without good listening skills. You have two ears and one mouth, this is a clue as to how much we should speak in contrast to how much we should listen. Yes, you got it! Listen twice as much. If people have said that you are fun to talk to, that's a good sign that you listen well and are on the right track.

Emotion drives logic. People do business with their friends and people they like. When others like you, they become more patient and tolerant of you. If my son makes a mess on the kitchen floor, am I going to kick him out of the house? No. But if an obnoxious stranger makes a mess, I will likely kick him out. Why? What's the difference? Relationship.

Emotional Language Barrier

It is hard enough at times to express our feelings in our native tongue; imagine trying to express yourself clearly in an unfamiliar language. Several years ago, I served a two-year mission in Brazil. The first three months were brutal. I had a hard time communicating, and I let it get to me.

The most difficult part was learning to express what I was feeling. I didn't realize the importance of **being understood** until no one could understand me. We all have an emotional need to be understood. I found that as I strived to understand what others were saying, they became more patient with me as I tried to communicate. You can quickly form strong relationships by seeking to understand and show patience in your interactions.

Cultural and language barriers may impede your ability to connect with your customers. Our first clients in Australia brought great opportunity and with it, some challenges. Our call monitors and coaches could not understand the calls between customer service reps and the customers. The words seemed to meld together. In fact, to comprehend each interaction, our coaches had to slow down each recording and replay it, over and over again. It was tedious work until we all became more comfortable with the accent.

You can learn a lot by actively listening to others. Instead of waiting for their lips to stop moving or thinking what you are going to say next, consider what they are saying. In a face-to-face interaction, you might lean forward, nod your head up and down, maintain eye contact, and even take notes. Over the phone, you can demonstrate good listening by using voice inflections, such as, *"hmmm," "oh my," "wow,"* or my personal favorite, *"woof."* You can rephrase or restate the information or ask additional questions. There are many ways to show you are engaged and are listening, but each one takes discipline and practice.

When you fill the emotional need to communicate and be understood, it creates a bond between speaker and listener—a connection that cultivates a relationship. Again, people do business with those they like. Learn to be more *interested* than *interesting.* Questions such as, *"tell me more?"* and *"what are you experiencing?"* are applications for active listening that have served me well. As long as I keenly listen to what is said next and become present to the expression, tone, and intent of others, the connections come naturally. Sadly, some that are successful in sales and service have yet to figure out the power of active listening. Take steps to ensure you are not one of them.

Question Mastery

Mastering the art of asking the right question(s) based on your understanding of a person's needs and wants, is a real art. It has to do with timing as well as an ability to pause and rephrase or reflect the speaker's intent. Great listeners can pinpoint the speaker's needs quickly. Some abuse the art to manipulate or control others. They endeavor to convince their customers that what they are selling will fulfill the customer's wants and needs, whether it's true or not. Some people use reflective listening for their own gain. But it is honorable to respect the gift and use the art with good intent.

You can tell the difference between manipulation and control, vs. persuasion and service by the way you feel after the interaction. If a course of action sounds good at the moment but afterward leaves you feeling unsettled or a little Caveat Emptor kicks in, it is likely that you experienced manipulation. If the salesperson is really good (but dishonorable), it can happen without you realizing. These kinds of feelings create hesitation to future interactions. On the other hand, if someone is actively listening to you and uses gentle persuasion to help you discover an option that will benefit you, the feeling during *and* after the exchange will be good.

Many people in business have incredible social skills and are very convincing. I have learned through experience that there is no in-between when it comes to what I will call, dishonorable practices. Lying, cheating and stealing is justified in the pursuit of money. In their minds, *"everyone does it."* Thankfully, I have not had to experience this type of sales very often as most of my interactions are with people who use this talent honorably and to serve others.

'Nice Bike'

I have experienced Mark Scharenbroich's gift for speaking twice. One of those times he spoke on making meaningful connections on the road of life. He moves people when he speaks. He makes them laugh. He makes them cry. He is also incredibly effective at persuading others to buy his book. At one of his events, I was able to introduce myself and tell him how I had enjoyed his speech at another venue. Next thing I know, I am summarizing my life story without even realizing it. I thought he was awesome, perhaps because I did all the talking. He walked the talk, being more *interested* than *interesting*.

When he spoke that night, he acknowledged me publicly along with several others in attendance. He presented us to the audience as if we were life-long friends. It was amazing! As he spoke, he connected in a very positive and personal way. That is an example of a powerfully persuasive listener. He was not in it for himself. He was genuine. I applied my own principles to our interaction. I felt great during his speech and with the things he shared, as well as afterward. No Caveat Emptor. He did not just listen—he showed sincere curiosity and interest. His expression of love made it difficult for me not to love him back.

You Must Be Present to Win

To create WOW Experiences and win the moment, you must stay cognitively aware during each customer interaction. How well do you understand and control your emotions? Are you aware of what you feel when your circumstance is abruptly altered? Can you recognize the emotions, whether happy, sad, angry, afraid or ashamed?

Understanding yourself seems like a no-brainer; after all, you have lived with yourself for many years. But *knowing yourself* is more than knowing your favorite food or hobbies. Knowing yourself is knowing how you react in certain situations, what you feel and why.

For example, think of the last time you experienced a strong reaction to something. What did you do? What did you feel? More importantly, what caused you to act and feel the way you did? Ask yourself these questions to become more self-aware and self-knowing. Learning about yourself and recognizing your emotions is one of the first steps to becoming present in your circumstances.

If you let yourself become distracted or caught up in your emotions, you miss the opportunities that may be present. Your capacity to meet the opportunity becomes impaired; in fact, you may not even see the opportunity to create a WOW Experience. If you can recognize the emotion and accept it for what it is or what it is trying to tell you, the recognition will enable you to move past the feeling. It doesn't mean you don't have the emotion, it just allows you to apply logic and consider the proper way to respond.

Your response must be disciplined and controlled—as opposed to responding by default triggers (what we call a knee-jerk reaction) that are tied to the emotion. For example, a few years ago, I was on a showroom floor at an event in Atlanta, unaware of the anger I was feeling towards my team for not performing as well as they should have. As I stood there stewing, one of my employees introduced me to a bigwig from a manufacturer that works with many of our clients.

After the brief interaction, my employee gently rebuked me for being cold and short and possibly harming a relationship he had been cultivating throughout the entire show. Because I did not quickly recognize the emotion I was experiencing, it made me blind to the opportunity before me. I did not even give myself a chance to win the moment because I was not present.

Being present, recognizing your emotions and setting your mind to serve others will enable you to seize the opportunities in front of you and take control of the outcome.

Open to Opportunity

My wife and I were ambitious early in our marriage. Her uncle owned a business selling cinnamon roasted almonds at events and shopping malls during the holidays. My wife and I would often rotate selling and cooking in the beginning. It was a lot of work, traveling to each of the shows, setting up, working from dawn until dusk for days, on up to six weeks straight. In time, I realized I preferred to do the selling. My wife could sell, too; but since I couldn't cook as well, she cooked the almonds.

With a little practice, we became a well-oiled machine! We took great pride in our work, and it showed. We had fun, and our customers had fun with us. One day in particular towards the end of a very long holiday event, I offered a gentleman a free sample. He initially declined, but I insisted. Soon we started talking, and he wondered why such a great salesperson was selling nuts in a mall. Towards the end of our conversation, he gave me his business card and invited me to his seminar later on during the week.

It turns out that the gentleman who gave me his card was none other than Jim Ackerman, an accomplished speaker, and writer. The seminar I attended was surprisingly excellent, and I wanted to be just like him. Jim's influence helped pave the way for how I provide for my family today. To win the moment, you must be present to the opportunity before you.

To become present, you need to create time for yourself. Make time every day to sit in a quiet place, alone, and allow yourself to think and ponder your feelings. Consider your daily circumstances from earlier and recognize how you acted. Did you respond the way you wanted? Did your response create the desired results? Or did the opposite occur? Record your thoughts and feelings in a journal.

A word of caution: While it's not a bad thing to think about and evaluate negative reactions, or times you displayed negative behavior, it is unfruitful to dwell on those situations and allow your inner critic free reign. Remember, this is a process to get to know yourself better and increase your confidence, not an exercise in self-deprecation. For example, if Michael Jordan had dwelled on being cut from the varsity basketball team, he would have never been present to the opportunity to improve and become arguably the greatest basketball player of all time. We should use our shortcomings as opportunities to learn and improve. As human beings, we naturally recognize weaknesses—in ourselves and others. In fact, we could spend day after day making a list of all the negative things we observe in those around us, but that won't help us become better. Remember that you can choose your experience independent of circumstance. Things happen that are outside of your control, but you can create innovative ways to observe, learn and respond accordingly.

Take Action: Operation "Self-Awareness"

Don't stop with just getting to know yourself better. While it's true that *knowing yourself* will increase your self-confidence, unless you take action, that new found confidence will be for not. As you learn how and why you react, look for ways to control those reactions.

Pushing the pause button on your emotional triggers while you work toward achieving a goal takes a disciplined response to events as they occur. Responding on purpose can be uncomfortable at times, but necessary to win the moment.

Identifying your emotions and reactions can lead to intentionally managing your actions in a positive way and achieving more success. In contrast, allowing your emotions to go unchecked will limit growth and therefore success. And unfortunately, unchecked emotions often have highly undesirable consequences.

Think about it. Who would you rather hire or promote—the person who is always calm and cool under pressure? Someone who puts others first and looks to what will benefit the company? Or the person who succumbs to their emotions, acting on impulse and having to correct mistakes caused by their rash behavior? No-brainer.

Six Questions to Get You Started

Here are six questions that will help you get started on your self-awareness journal to become present and win the moment.

1. *Do you have enough energy?* Do you engage in your work with positive enthusiasm? Do you feel enjoyment doing what you do?
2. *Do you define yourself by criteria other than work?* Picture yourself like a pie. How big of a bite does your work take out of your pie?
3. *Do you have a positive self-image?* Obsessive passion is associated with a negative self-image, including unpleasant feelings about yourself.
4. *When you work, is your internal dialogue positive?* Do you use words like "*want to,*" "*get to*" and "*can't wait to*"; or do your thoughts focus on "*must,*" "*need*" and "*have to?*"
5. *Can you stop working when you want to?* People who are harmoniously passionate about work feel positive emotions while working. Obsessive workers feel more negative both while working *and* when prevented from work. Do you feel the compulsion to work all the time, even when you don't need to?
6. *Do you get into the flow?* Do you feel like time has receded into the background when you work, or do you feel a weight on your shoulders? Flow allows an enjoyable experience, whereas obsessive engagement feels more urgent.

By knowing yourself and your emotions, you can manage your reactions to circumstance. This allows you to be present; not pulled to and fro by your emotions. Being present allows you to be a better listener, both to others and to yourself. And by being present and listening, you open yourself up to the opportunities that present themselves. Remember, *you must be present to win*!

To create WOW Experiences, discipline yourself to stay intimately engaged in the moment. As you learn to listen and connect with others by remaining present to their expression, tone, and intent, you will learn about them and their needs, which will increase your value and inspire you to action. As long as you are aware, you can act autonomously to address the customer's wants/needs and create unique value that will WOW them. To WOW more, listen more. To win the moment, put forth the effort to become a better listener. If you have not made an entry already in your journal, now's a very good time. Are you present? What do you know and believe about active listening? How about seeking first to understand or being more self-aware? What steps can you take to become a better and more active listener? Articulate your answers on paper and draw up a plan to create better listening habits in your life.

7 Principle 4: Care Respect Individual Worth

Others can connect and become present as we show genuine empathy and respect for their worth

Pre-assessment question: Are you socially aware of others and their need for you to care?

Others can better connect with you and be present as you show genuine empathy and respect for their worth. In this chapter, you will learn to influence your emotional state of being, independent of circumstance and outside forces, to show others that you care.

In America, we champion freedom. Of course, there are several free countries around the world, but few are as proud of their freedom or celebrate their freedom more than Americans. Freedom is part of who we are as a nation. Learning to embody the Pattern for Excellence takes freedom to a whole new level where you can do your best work. Why? Because you can empathize with others and help them see past their emotion to uncover a viable solution that alleviates their weight or burden. Our freedom and peace of mind are more deeply felt as we sincerely empathize and carry one another's burdens.

Empathy Shows Caring

I was working with a team in Ohio, and my wife began to call my cell phone. She knew I was training that day and doesn't usually reach out unless something has gone wrong. When I called her back, she blew right past our usual felicities at the beginning of our call and sternly began the conversation with, "Your son"… and I knew I was in trouble! "Your son just wiped baby rash cream all over your new flat-screen TV," she vented.

Now I could have replied by saying, "Why aren't you watching my son?" But that would have put me in the doghouse, right? Luckily, what I said was, "That's terrible! I can't imagine why he would do such a thing. I wish I were there."

"I know, this always happens when you are not here," she responded. As I continued empathizing, she was able to talk through it and get it off her chest. I gave her the opportunity to connect with me because I showed genuine concern for her situation and validated her frustration. At times we tend to jump in and begin problem-solving when it would be more effective first to empathize with the other frustrated party. It shows that you care about what they are experiencing.

Most people are smart enough to find solutions to overcome their adversity. What keeps them from those solutions are the emotions they feel when the adversity occurs. If you can help them work through those emotions, you validate their worth and help carry that burden with them, enabling the other party to think clearly and come up with a solution or find a way to move forward.

Empathy is the ability within us to identify with, understand, and appreciate one another. Expressing sincere empathy with others may not come naturally for you, but that's OK. Much like the muscles in your body, empathy can be enhanced. I would caution you, however, that practicing empathy is essential to avoid sounding contrived. It is difficult to recover and connect with others if your interaction with them is plagued with insincerity. No one trusts a person who comes across as fake.

The best way to express empathy consistently is simply to show that you sincerely care. Showing others kindness and caring is hard enough when you already have a connection with them but showing care and concern for someone you don't know or don't have a connection with is even harder. As you learn to express genuine empathy, you'll see the difference it makes in your effort to create WOW Experiences. Start practicing today!

Choosing not to feel or engage in relationships is one of the main reason marriages, families, and friendships fail. Partners blame infidelity on being ignored or forgotten. Kids say they acted out because their parents didn't seem to care or did not try to understand their feelings. Friends have misunderstandings, and when they do not bother to work through them, they end the friendship, or it withers and dies. In all three of these cases, an emotional need wasn't fulfilled. Thus, they went elsewhere to fill the void. I am not condoning such actions, but merely stating a fact that emotions motivate action. Emotions are very real and should be taken seriously with care and genuine concern.

We are meant to carry one another's burdens as well as have our burdens carried. An inability or choice to be unempathetic impedes your capacity to connect and share the adversity or pain that those burdens create. The weight we feel in the face of our adversity is bondage. We feel trapped and cannot see through our emotions. Some people become so hardened in response to their adversity that they cannot feel at all, either to help others or to share their own burden. Emotional bondage is one reason why we may act out of character and fail to empathize during hard times.

Sincere empathy helps you feel one another's burden and makes the burden lighter for others. Empathy provides emotional strength to assist in seeing circumstances more clearly, finding answers and responding accordingly to enable you to move past adversity. Human beings by nature are a social species. Our survival depends on interpersonal relationships where we express and accept empathy. By recognizing this reality and embracing it, you help yourself become a valuable asset to your spouse, children, friends and to those in which we come in contact.

You may think that by engaging in empathy, your interactions might get off track or take too much time. You may also feel uncomfortable when others share their personal stories. Receiving too much information—such as the medications others take or recent surgeries or situations involving close friends or family— might make you cringe. But learning about uncomfortable situations is part of the human experience. Others need your help to carry their emotional load. As you learn to connect in this way, people will feel more comfortable interacting with you. Yes, small tangents may side-track conversation, but by asking the right questions, you can keep the conversation on track while showing sincere concern.

Here is a helpful tool to assist in replacing cliché words like "sorry" and "okay."

Relate to their situation:	• I have had that happen to me before • That's happening a lot lately
Use an expression of concern:	• Hmmm • Oh no • Wow • Geez • Goodness me! • Woof!
Agree to the gravity of their situation:	• That's not good • That's horrible • That's terrible • I hate to hear that
Feel for their circumstance:	• I can only imagine what you are going through right now

In many cases, the situation that is shared can be of a serious nature. Using the Care principle in such scenarios manifests your competence in handling these situations. Use your empathic listening skills to discern their expression, tone, and intent—and respond accordingly.

Sometimes people may seem like they are angry at you, as if you were personally involved in the thing that upset them. Keep in mind that few people wake up in the morning deciding they are going to treat others poorly. In these situations, learn to put your emotions aside. Do not react to them, rather learn to control your tendency to treat others the way they are treating you. Maintain your focus on active listening and expressing sincere empathy.

Don't Get Offended

Sooner or later, someone will do or say something that could be considered offensive. As you begin to master the Listening and Care principles, you will become more socially aware and more easily recognize such instances. One of the greatest indicators of mastery in the Pattern for Excellence is in how we respond to the ignorant and inexperienced actions of others.

When others say or do something that you consider offensive, choose not to take offense. Believing that someone or something can make you feel a particular way—whether it be bitter, sad, offended, hurt, unworthy or angry—makes you an object to be acted upon as opposed to choosing how you respond and act proactively in potentially offensive or hurtful situations.

Although others may not intentionally offend you, they can be inconsiderate or rash in their communication. Whether inadvertently or not, others may treat you as an object, especially in business. If a customer does not appreciate the service provided or product delivered, you may find yourself as the one to whom they air their grievance. If they treat you poorly, and you fail to recognize their worth as an individual with feelings and valid emotions, you may react or fall into the same pattern of poor behavior as they are exhibiting. They are upset, and they are reacting to that emotion.

You can recognize the emotion felt and express empathy without admitting blame.

Effective listening often helps defuse tense situations because most reasonable people tend to soften up when they see that they are talking to an actual person who understands them and cares about what they're experiencing. This realization can often change their disposition towards you, and they'll begin to treat you more kindly.

Empathize with Upset Customers

When a customer is not satisfied with your service or has a complaint about you (for example, if a customer is calling with a complaint that is legitimate to them, by extension, it should also be legitimate to you), there are several options for how you can react. Keep in mind that your response will likely affect your long-term relationship with that customer. Choose to respond proactively with your end goal in mind.

Here are some of the best choices in service recovery situations. Empathize with them. People respond to empathy because it does two things: 1) it shows you are listening and that you identify with the problem because you have experienced something similar or that you can imagine how it would feel to have that problem, and 2) it builds a bridge of trust between you and the customer. When people feel understood, they become more trusting. When people feel more trusting, they are more open to the solutions you provide. Always ensure that you are expressing empathy when the customer is upset.

Apologize when you or your company has wronged them. Sometimes just recognizing that something went wrong and offering a sincere apology for the slip-up is enough to begin changing a potentially bad situation into a positive experience. Everybody makes mistakes; it's good to admit them when you do.

Do something unexpected. This goes hand-in-hand with offering an apology. Your apology can only go so far; you need to follow that up by providing a solution. That solution should be something unexpected. Sometimes, simply giving them what they want can be unexpected, at least for some businesses. But yours is not just some business—yours is the best customer service business out there! Not only do you want to satisfy the customer, but you want to take it one step further. Send them a hand-written note, call them a few days later to follow up, go the extra mile based on their specific wants and needs; do something they simply do not expect.

By expressing sincere empathy and apologizing, you start correcting the situation and restoring trust. Doing something extra or unexpected to take care of your customer can turn a bad experience into a positive experience that customers will remember, and they'll come back for more. They will also likely tell their friends, and their friends will come and do business with you. Because of your positive response to a mistake, you may win many new customers.

Empathy: Understand First

A prayer that has been quoted many times, originally written by St. Francis of Assisi says, "*Seek first to understand, then to be understood.*" This is poignant advice to anyone, but it is of particular importance to those in the relationship-building business. How many times can you recall having a problem with a company just because they assumed they knew your situation? It happens all too frequently, and unless we have no other option, you don't return to the offending company.

For example, last Christmas I was shopping for a new computer for my mom. She works on a second-generation iMac; and while it's still a great computer, it was aging. I was sure I was going to get her another Mac, but out of curiosity, I stopped by our local PC store.

When I entered, I was immediately approached and asked what I was looking for and how the service person could help. I explained that I was looking for a mid-grade computer—nothing too fancy—for my mom and was wondering what they had. The sales guy showed me a couple of models and started talking about their capabilities. He asked what my mom needed, and I started by explaining that we were predominantly Mac users, and that is what she was accustomed to using. Without letting me finish, he interrupted and said, "Oh, and let me guess, do you or your mom drive a Subaru? You know, because they are so trendy too?"

I was floored. I was about to explain that I had heard such good things about their computers and that I thought I would come in and see if they were a good fit for my mom. Instead, I never got the chance to finish, and the sales guy never got the chance to sell a computer. Needless to say, I have no plans of returning and I am telling all my friends about my bad experience!

Let people finish what they want to say. Sure, they may take a little longer to get it out, but do yourself a favor—let them finish. And once they finish, show that you have paid attention by rephrasing what was said. You'll be amazed at how appreciative they are that you gave them a chance to speak. It shows them you care and makes them feel important. Remember the definition of the Care principle: *Others can connect and become present as we show genuine empathy and respect for their worth. That's how relationships are built.*

By listening and rephrasing what you heard, you might learn something that the person was unable to articulate clearly at first and propose options that they hadn't even considered. You might even be able to help them solve a problem they didn't know they had! You see, they will listen to you because you first listened to them. They'll listen because they know you understand what they need. Showing them you're listening will help them trust you and increase their confidence in you and your company. And as they begin to trust and like you, chances are they'll buy from you, refer their friends to you and come back and buy more in the future.

Don't let yourself get distracted by other phone calls, emails or text messages. The person you are speaking with should hold your complete attention. They'll sense it if you become distracted. Seek to understand them truly and by doing so, you'll build your customer's confidence, and without question, WOW more customers.

Since effective communication is key to your success in building relationships, you need to read your customer's disposition at the start of your interaction. Do you know when to let the conversation flow and when to interject to move the conversation along? Do you have a plan you have practiced thoroughly and can follow that will help you know how to act regardless of the client's disposition? If not, you should; having a plan will help you WOW more customers.

We all recognize what happens to our feelings when things go wrong. Therefore, it makes sense that we can also understand that when a client calls, they are looking for a solution to their situation. To reassure customers that they have come to the right place and immediately build their trust, your team must be able to empathize with your customer's plight.

Empathy plays a crucial role in customer service, and the capacity to recognize a customer's concerns and connect with them on an emotional level has proven time and again to be an important factor in a brand's reputation and bottom line.

Two Ways to Start Empathizing

Once in a communications class at college my professor explained that when we communicate, we are sometimes like butchers and other times we are like fire-hydrants. There are times, he explained, when we have a problem to talk about, all we want to do is talk. We don't need an answer; we just need to spout, like a fire hydrant. At other times, we need to play butcher and chop our problems into pieces so we can evaluate and solve them one by one.

Start practicing these two ways to empathize with your customers now:

Fire-hydrant mode. If you have a home service company, start your call by finding out why the customer is calling. Let them know you care and are listening by asking questions about their problem. Their response will indicate their attitude.

The following exchange between a CSR and customer illustrates how this works.

CSR: "Thanks for calling ABC Repair. This is Joe, how can I help you?"

Customer: "Yeah, Joe, I'm having a problem with my drains. They are clogged, and nothing I have done seems to be working."

CSR: "Oh, that's no good. Tell me a little more about what's happening. Which drains are we talking about?"

Customer: "It's the drains in my kitchen sink and my main bathroom. You know, the shower and sink both don't drain. I don't know what it is; I just got out of the shower this morning, and they were all stopped up. I tried plunging, running hot water, running one of those little clog-removal things you can get at Home Depot, but nothing worked. They're all still plugged. I don't want to try any Drano or anything like that because I don't want it just pooling in my sink, you know? I don't have any idea what it could be; everything drained just fine last night; it's just this morning that there's been a problem. I wonder if a pipe could be frozen or something; is that possible?"

CSR: "That may be. So if I understand you right, the issue is with the drains in your bathroom sink and shower, as well as your kitchen sink?"

Customer: "That's it. And man, they just…nothing. No draining at all. Even when I plunge, nothing. I don't know what it could be."

CSR: "Wow. I can only imagine what you're going through right now. We can definitely help. When would you like us to come out?"

In this example, it's clear the customer is distressed and is in more of a fire-hydrant mode. He's running through potential issues and solutions on his own, and so all the CSR needs to do is listen, show empathy and ask for the appointment.

Butcher Mode. In this example, the customer's communication is in butcher mode.

CSR: "Thanks for calling ABC Repair. This is Joe. How may I help you?"

Customer: "Hi, I need someone to come fix my drains."

CSR: "Alright, we can definitely help you with that. Can you tell me a little more about what's happening?"

Customer: "Yeah, the drains in my kitchen sink and my bathroom aren't draining."

CSR: "Oh, that is terrible. How long have they been plugged?"

Customer: "Just since this morning."

CSR: "Hmm, that's not good. So the drains were working fine yesterday?"

Customer: "Yes, no problem at all. But I have standing water in both sinks and my tub this morning."

CSR: "That's not fun."

Customer: "Yeah, I tried plunging and got no results. I don't really want to try chemicals, especially in my kitchen sink."

CSR: "I understand, and I don't blame you; I wouldn't want Drano in my kitchen sink either. Okay, so if I understand, you have clogged drains in your kitchen sink as well as in your bathroom sink and tub. You have tried plunging with no effect and the drains appeared to work fine last night?"

Customer: "Yep, that's pretty much it."

CSR: "We can certainly get that fixed for you. When would you like us to come out?"

When the customer's communication is in butcher mode, the CSR needs to ask more questions to get the customer talking about his situation.

Again, people like to do business with their friends—and it's easier to relate to those who have a similar communication style (or at least with those who can recognize and communicate in their preferred communication style). So if from the start of the call, you can determine if a person is in a hydrant mode versus a butcher mode and respond accordingly, the customer will feel more comfortable with you and act friendlier towards you. And once you have a customer who is a friend, you have a much better chance of creating a WOW Experience. Work on your ability to perceive your customer's disposition at the beginning of your interaction together and handle it accordingly.

A Stern Rebuke

I met Mr. Dewey Jenkins of Morris Jenkins (a reputable company in North Carolina) at an event several years ago. We hit it off during a breakout session, and he gave me permission to talk business when he got back to his offices in Charlotte. Two weeks later, I sent Mr. Jenkins an email that said something like this:

"Dewey, you and I met at an event a couple of weeks ago. We're the ones that train teams how to create WOW Experiences for their customers. We'll be close to Charlotte in a few weeks and would like to train your team while we're there. We're the best at what we do. How does the first week in November look for us to come out and train your team?"

To say that I was soon embarrassed at the presumptuous tone I took in my email is an understatement. What was amazing however, was the show of maturity and experience that Mr. Jenkins demonstrated in his response. He simply replied, "Brigham, you've asked for the order without even doing a warm-up. I'm not that easy. I deserve more respect."

He could have ignored my email or responded in the same tone. Instead, Mr. Jenkins chose a different tact. Although stern in his rebuke, he left the door open for me to answer for the disrespect I had shown him.

My response was somewhat like this, "Mr. Jenkins, you're right—you do deserve more respect! I meant no disrespect, so please forgive me. Would you be open to letting me show you how we work via webinar? All I would need is 10 minutes, or I could come and visit you and your team when I'm in town in a couple of weeks. Which feels more comfortable to you?"

Mr. Jenkins was right—he did deserve more respect, but he chose not to be offended and enabled me to see my error and correct it. It was a privilege to interact with him and his team. I am so grateful for the example he set for me as well as the opportunity later to train his team.

When we believe or say we are offended, we usually mean we feel insulted, mistreated or disrespected. In reality, it is impossible for anyone else to offend you or me. Believing that another person offended us is categorically incorrect. To be offended is a choice we make—not a condition inflicted or imposed on us by others.

John C. Maxwell declared, "Nothing is truly a mistake unless you don't learn from it." Leaders must be learners if they want to keep leading. Where there is a mistake, accept responsibility and take steps to both improve and move forward as the leader of your organization.

Instead of being offended, choose to take the lead in creating WOW Experiences by keeping your emotions out of it so others can be free to express their emotions and work through them. It is a common belief that you should "put yourself in someone else's shoes" to understand them completely. When you do this, ensure that you are seeing their situation from their perspective, rather than seeing their situation from your perspective. Each of us may respond differently in similar situations. Give others the opportunity to connect by becoming present and showing genuine empathy and respect for their worth. To create a WOW Experience, you must care by showing them that you can feel what they are feeling.

Alright, you should know the drill by now. Write down what you know to be true about this principle. Consider personal experiences or stories you've heard that relate to this principle. Articulate an action plan that will help you form habits that will show customers that you care.

8

Principle 5: Say "Yes" Give Beyond Expectation

We give first to create WOW Experience and build long-term relationships

Pre-assessment questions : How do you first give to create WOW Experiences and build long-term relationships?

Customers tend to mirror what we say and do in our interactions. When we say "no," they say "no." When we say "Yes," the customer often says "Yes" as well.

Suppose your customers are not sure about you or your company. If your first few answers to their questions contain word phrases such as, "we don't" or "I don't know," what the customer hears is that you cannot help them. The fact remains that you can help them if you really wanted to, even if the help you provide does not directly benefit you or your company.

Thanks to Google, you never have to say the words, "I don't know" again. So why would you go out of your way to help customers even if it does not directly benefit you? This is what saying "Yes" is all about. When you help them first, whether it benefits you directly or not, customers will be more inclined to reach out to you first in the future. Give first to create a WOW Experience and build a long-term relationship whether it benefits you directly or not. Once you provide the help the customer needs, there is a better chance they'll work with you later.

Have you ever focused more on what you can do as opposed to what you cannot do? Have you ever thought about saying "Yes," even if it is something you do not offer? When you discipline yourself always to say "Yes," you will be surprised at how much you can do for customers. When you learn to listen and care about customers, you will become aligned with what they need and want. Finding answers to their needs and wants will be easier to come by when you learn to always say, "Yes." Life is sales! So learn to say "Yes" more often, and others will reciprocate.

We all love YES!

It was a big day for me almost 20 years ago—June 10th to be exact. I was going to ask for my wife's hand in marriage. The ring was all picked out. The setting I chose was beautiful, and I was ready to go. I gave her several subtle hints that it was going to happen.

What am I looking for her to say when I pop the big question? That's right, I am looking for her to say "Yes!" wholeheartedly. I wanted my investment of time and effort to pay off! Of course, I desperately wanted her to say "Yes."

The same thing happens with my kids. When I ask them to clean their room, I want them to say, "Yes." When I'm at a restaurant, and I'm asked if I want more bacon, of course, I'm going to say, "Yes." You see, we all want to hear the word, "Yes."

However, when we talk to customers, we tend to say "no" words—such as, "we don't, that's not possible, we can't, there is no way, unfortunately," etc. What should you say? Say "Yes!" When you begin with "Yes," the tendency of the customer is to reciprocate.

Here is one example of an exchange between a customer and a CSR.

Customer: "Hi, I am looking for a ballpark price on an air conditioner."

CSR: "Great, tell me more about your situation?"

Customer: "I woke up this morning to a warm house, and my home only got hotter as the day wore on."

CSR: "Oh, that's not good."

Customer: "I know, not fun."

CSR: "We can definitely help you with that. When would you like us to come out?"

Customer: "This afternoon would work great."

Regardless of what your customer asks for, create a WOW Experience by focusing only on what you can do for the customer. Always say, "Yes" in one way or another.

Imagine Saying Yes

Imagine that you just got a hot tip from a very credible source that guarantees you'll win the billion-dollar Power Ball lottery this weekend. The winning lottery ticket is a short four-hour drive outside of town, and so you have to figure out a way to sneak out and get that ticket. The only downside is that your favorite nephew asked you to be at his birthday party, and your boss said he would write you up if you missed your 12-hour weekend shift again. So it's really not the best time to drive four hours outside of town based on a tip, no matter how credible the source. I would bet, however, that you'll still figure out a way to get that lottery ticket—no matter the level of difficulty.

I realize that this example is extreme, but my point is this: Your customers call you because they want and need your help. The question is, what lengths are you willing to go to exceed their expectation? What risks will you take? What will you do to deliver service in a way the customer did not expect? Your goal is to create a WOW Experience, and you can't do that if you say, "no."

There are, of course, limitations to what you can do, and I'm not asking you to make promises you cannot keep. Just focus in on what you can do and reassure the customer that you can help because there is always something you can do if you are creative enough to consider the possibilities.

PRINCIPLE 5: SAY "YES"

The word "Yes" is very powerful. When you use "Yes," it means that something is going to get done. It puts people and things in motion. When you set goals, you also imply that you're going to move forward. You are saying "Yes" to those goals. That means that something is going to change.

When you ask for the sale, you hope your customer will say "Yes." When you ask your girlfriend for her hand in marriage, you anticipate that she is going to say "Yes." When you ask your kid to clean his room, you hope that he not only says "Yes" but actually does it!

Saying "Yes" often leads to an unexpected outcome. Have you ever seen the 2008 movie *Yes Man*, starring Jim Carrey? Within the movie, Jim Carrey's character is stuck in a rut. He attends a self-help seminar and although he is forced to say "Yes" to everything, he learns to unleash the power of saying YES, which of course leads him down a path of incredible transformation.

This movie shows us how saying "Yes" can be of tremendous value. Apply that to the business world and the results multiply. The more we say "Yes," the more we will hear "Yes."

Below is an application of words and phrases we do not want to use, in fact, remove them from your vocabulary entirely. You want your customer to hear that you will do everything you can to meet their needs. Focus on what you can do to help and reassure the customer that they're in good hands.

Application Examples: Seek to Give First

This list provides words and word phrases you should not use:

Unfortunately	I/We can try
Let's see	There's no way
Sorry	No
I/We can't	I don't know
That's not possible	I can't help you

It takes practice and discipline to avoid using these words and phrases; however, once you master the ability to reassure customers that they've called the right place at the start of the call and the ability to focus on what you can do, you will WOW more customers. You will be able to create a positive experience that they did not anticipate. Say "Yes" and your customers will reciprocate—they, too, will say "Yes!"

Sometimes in business, we have a "me first" mentality. I have experienced it in the past, and it has gotten me absolutely nowhere. I learned out of desperation that giving first will make all the difference when you put your needs aside for others and use your listening skills to find out what people really need and want. Seek to give first to create WOW experiences and build long-term relationships.

My First Sales Job

During my college years, I had a sales job that was challenging. I had a co-worker who expressed his concern by saying, "If we can't make sales together then we can't work together."

What a bunch of baloney! If you believe that what you're doing will benefit others, then don't let the lack of sales stop you. Figure out a different way to sell it!

All you have to do is find an opportunity to share your talents with others. You might offer to do it for free. Make them see the value of what you offer. Giving first, without the expectation of payment, opens doors. It shows that your motives and intentions are rooted in your belief that the work you do is of great worth. People will not only see what you do, but they will see why you do it—if you give first without expectation. As author Simon Sinek stated, "People don't buy what you do—they buy why you do it."

When I first started my coaching company, I only had a few clients—barely enough to get by. Among them was the owner of a company who did not feel the need to maintain my coaching services. What made it difficult was that he wasn't directly involved in the coaching process and had no idea how much change had occurred and how the success of his call center had increased. I needed to act quickly to rectify this situation and maintain his account.

My plan was to give first to create a WOW Experience and fast. I spoke with the company's general manager about developing a training manual for his office staff that he could use for future training purposes. I also offered to train his field staff the next time I came into his office. He liked the idea, so we began to consider some training topics.

By the time the meeting was over, I had offered an on-site training and all at no extra charge. I left my client's office knowing I had increased my shelf life for at least another month or two. I also was keenly aware that I had better be ready to perform when I got back because I wouldn't get another shot. It was a sink-or-swim situation, which is why my preparation began on the flight home. Once I completed the manual, I had a 12-page prototype for my client's office staff and I was prepared to provide training to his field staff.

The owner of the company attended the field staff training to get to know me and my training style. He then began to see more value in having me around long-term, and it increased my shelf life. I was invited back to train his field staff several times over the following months. I continued to provide the service without hesitation and at no charge.

The owner attended every training, each time giving me an opportunity to show him my capacity and value. He soon began to give me advice on how to make the field staff training better (it's always a good sign when your client gives you pointers and advice). If he didn't believe in my capacity to provide value to him and his team, he would not have wasted his breath to help me improve the training. Always be grateful for feedback—good, bad or indifferent. Silence is the only time you should be concerned about your position. If you're not getting feedback, start asking questions; your job could very well be in jeopardy.

Yes, the manual helped the office staff and writing it helped me refine my thoughts and training practices, but I'm not so sure it helped me keep my job as much as the free field staff training. By giving first, writing the manual and providing the group training, I was honing my skills as a coach and enhancing my ability to offer more value to my clients. I was able to create a WOW Experience and build a long-term relationship.

Things have a way of working out as long as you say "Yes" to opportunity, exercise faith and put forth the effort to make the most of it. To create WOW Experiences, say "Yes" and give first, beyond expectation.

Write down what you know to be true about this principle. Consider personal experiences or stories you have heard that confirm your belief in the "Yes" principle. Articulate a game plan to put what you know and believe into action.

9

Principle 6: Ask-If You Don't Ask, You Don't Get

We are accountable to clarify what is missing,
learn the right answers and respond accordingly

Pre-assessment question: Are your customer responses intentional
and disciplined to create WOW Experiences?

W e are all customers, but we are also all different and have different wants and needs. You may be good at treating others the way *you* want to be treated; however, you cannot assume to know how *they* want to be treated. To learn what your clients want, you need to get a clear understanding by asking good questions, zeroing in on the right answer and autonomously responding.

There's that word again, *autonomous*. Its meaning is so fundamentally important that I can't use it enough. All the processes and scripts in the world cannot replace the autonomous actions you develop with practice and the belief that you are providing a vital service. For a WOW Experience to occur, the way in which you serve must come from the heart. It cannot be faked or contrived. Asking questions that clarify how you can best serve your customers create opportunities so you can WOW them. That is what the Pattern for Excellence is all about. Mastering the art of clarifying questions is key to creating value for your clients.

First, you might ask yourself, *"What is lacking in our company?"* Have you considered asking your team the same question? I take my executive team away six full days a year to answer that one simple question. We are constantly evolving as an organization and are aligned because we work together to answer important questions like *"What's missing in our business, and how can we do better?"*

Our company vision, purpose, mission and core values are created at these executive get-a-ways. Vital improvement to our processes and procedures has come from the time we dedicate to working *on* the business together not just *in* the business. It is so important to consider the obstacles or events that affect our business and decide together how to respond to produce the outcome we desire. Once we have clarity, we become collectively intentional and disciplined in our responses.

Try Should Lead to *Buy*

Here's a way to think about achieving your desired outcome—more sales, right?

Asking should lead to answers. Companies have become excellent at answering questions. Employees have so much product knowledge these days that they can answer most customers' questions with little hesitation. They have mastered answering questions—not just in-person, but over the phone, online, via email, social chats, and texting.

Answers should lead to trying. I find it remarkable that call handling teams will sit and answer every question under the sun over the phone, and when all the questions are answered, the customer says, "Wow, you've been great! I am going to disconnect now and think about this for a while and who knows, I might reach back out to you."

Trying should lead to buying. What just happened? Your end goal is to create a WOW Experience! How can you do that if your customer receives answers but then does not have the opportunity even to try, let alone buy, your product or service?

Green Eggs and Ham

Let us consult the greatest sales book of all time, *Green Eggs and Ham*, written by Dr. Seuss. In this classic children's book, Sam is trying to get this grumpy old guy to try green eggs and ham. He pulls out all the stops. He would ask, *"Would you like them on a boat with a goat or in a box with a fox?"*

Sam is relentless! He is bound and determined to convince this guy to at least try green eggs and ham. Finally, the guy says, *"Sam, if you will let me be, I will try them, you will see."*

Sam is ecstatic that his determination and persistence has paid off. When the taste test is over, the grumpy old guy proclaims that he would eat green eggs and ham *"anywhere"* because he loves them so much.

You see my point? The WOW Experience does not occur until the guy tries or "buys" green eggs and ham! When you are talking to customers and answering their questions, don't forget to ask your own questions. Like Sam, ask your customers to *try* your product or service so they can experience it—and then to *buy* your product so they can continue the WOW Experience you create.

The one who asks the questions is the one who ultimately controls the outcome of the interaction. If you let customers drive by only answering their questions, you lower your chances of creating WOW Experiences because the customer walks away without buying the experience you want to create. To create more WOW Experiences, ask more questions. Ask early, and ask often. That Sam-I-Am, That Sam-I-Am. Oh, how I LOVE that Sam-I-Am. Thank you, thank you, Dr. Seuss!

Autonomous Work

Arriving home late one night from a business trip, I had missed dinner by at least three hours. My eight-year-old daughter, Bela, was the only one still up. As I looked through my refrigerator, I noticed that I had everything I needed to make my "Brazilian Salad." I cut tomatoes and cucumbers into small pieces, placed them in a bowl, added real lime juice, olive oil, salt, and a pinch of cayenne pepper. I learned how to make this salad on a recent trip to Brazil.

Deciding to enjoy my salad while watching TV, I walked over to the family room, plopped down on the couch and turned on a show. Bela soon sat down next to me and reached out her hand, presuming I would share. I abruptly said "no."

She already had some of the same salad for dinner, and now she wanted mine too! Determined to have some of my salad, she brought a bowl of her own and asked me to share. She was more polite in asking on the second attempt, which softened me up a little, but my answer was still, "no."

Bela was persistent. She continued to ask in new and creative ways, yet was also cautious by remaining polite and not pushing me too hard. She then delivered a pitch that sold me. "Dad, give me two slices of tomatoes and three slices of cucumber, and I will leave you alone to watch your show."

I was so impressed with her gutsy and innovative proposal that I accepted her offer. I couldn't help but feel great pride for her ingenuity and her refusal to take "no" for an answer. Although perturbed in the beginning, I was persuaded to say "yes" and felt good about our transaction in the end. Bela had considered the obstacle before her and became clear on what she wanted. This clarity along with the right questions turned my "no" into a "yes." Her actions were calculated and intentional, based on the outcome she desired. I just wish I knew where she gets it!

Persistence Pays Dividends

In selling situations, I've learned not to settle for "*maybe*," I'm looking for a "*yes*" or a "*no*" and I'm willing to persist until I get one or the other. Even when a customer says "*no,*" it may only mean "*not right now.*" Some sales take longer than others. I've had some sales take over a year to close. Once made, the client always compliments me on my persistence.

By asking the right questions you help others to clarify what is missing, to discover the outcome they want, and then you can ask more of the right questions that will motivate your customer to make a purchase. WOW Experiences don't happen if your client does not buy your product or service.

Similar to the *Listen* principle, asking the right questions can make you very persuasive. On the other hand, misuse can result in control and manipulation. Remember that your goal is to create WOW Experiences and build long-term relationships. That won't happen if you try to offer something that your customer does not want or need. You might make them feel good in the moment, but later they will regret their decision and may even come to resent you and your company.

As you work toward opportunities to create WOW, learn to probe effectively to understand what's important to others. As you listen to understand and express empathy when appropriate, practice pausing as needed. Filling the silence in your conversations often "talks" the customer out of making a commitment to buy. Remember, two ears and one mouth? When you are patient and quiet at the right time, it will enable others to work through the opportunity you present and consider their best options without interruption. Just sit quietly and let them work through the matter and you will be surprised how often they resolve it on their own.

Mastering the *Ask* principle will teach you to ask the right questions. It helps whomever you are speaking with to weigh their options without pressure and gives them the freedom to discover what is right for them. You create WOW Experiences by being altruistic and asking questions that will truly benefit the customer. Once they have solidified what they feel is the best course of action, having considered your thought-provoking questions, they can clearly see the appropriate path and respond accordingly. Mastery of the ASK principle separates the good from the great in persuasive selling.

Getting Out of the Way

While training a call handling team in Columbus, Ohio, I answered some of their customer calls and showed them how to sell service agreements over the phone. One customer, Mrs. Lawson, sounded like Wanda Sykes over the phone. She was older and had a lot of spunk.

She called the company for the third time in six weeks because her heating and cooling system still wasn't working correctly. You wouldn't think this was an optimal time to sell a service agreement, but I felt it was the best option based on her needs.

I reviewed her notes and made her aware that we visited her home several times over the past three years. I asked her why she did not have a service agreement with us. She said, "It's not worth it. For the money I have paid you thus far, I want to see results."

I assured her that she would absolutely experience a positive result and that the only reason why I brought up the service agreement is that it would save her 20% off all our services, plus she would never have to pay another dispatch fee again.

She explained that she did not have the budget at the moment but needed A/C in her home. The more I actively listened to her predicament, the more she shared with me. Her husband just had hip replacement surgery and suffered from periodic aneurisms. I expressed empathy and continued to listen. When she paused for a breath, I reassured her that the service agreement would save her money. She abruptly interrupted me and said, "So what you are saying is the service agreement will save me money even though it doesn't sound like it does."

I paused for a moment and reassured her that it would save her money. After another brief moment, she asked, "Well, how much would I have to pay for it?" As I explained how payments worked and told her I could get it all set up right over the phone, she consulted with her husband and decided to move forward with a service agreement.

What just happened? In the beginning, there was nothing I could say that would make her change her mind. The service agreement was not worth the cost to her until I showed her I was listening and that I sincerely cared about her and her husband. Selling became easy as I actively listened to her and showed her I sincerely cared. She then became comfortable and open to my idea. I just needed to get out of her way. This is the Pattern for Excellence in action.

As I became present to her expression, tone, and intent, she could sense that I cared and that I respected her worth. Had I not done so, she would have stuck to her guns and felt that I did not understand her or that I was just trying to make her buy something she didn't need.

Understanding your customer's point of view and showing that you recognize their emotions helps them be open to your logic and to look at the options presented. There was a paradigm shift that happened, and it was Mrs. Lawson that made the shift, I just helped her along. I listened and cared, which made her feel understood and comforted. She felt safe and could consider what made the most sense for her without feeling like I was selling her something. Once she realized what made the most sense, I simply invited her to respond accordingly.

Persuasion occurs when you have the best interest of your customer in mind. You help them clarify what is missing, discover the right answers and invite them to respond accordingly. You might think that these principles are common sense, and that may be true, but they are definitely not common practice. What we lack are mastery and *action*. When you ask the right questions, you can make the "action" the customer's idea—not just your idea. *Asking* becomes a powerful tool that helps them discover what is missing and make course corrections they freely choose.

Albert Einstein wisely noted: "If I had an hour to solve a problem and my life depended on the solution, I would spend the first 55 minutes determining the proper question to ask, for once I know the proper question, I could solve the problem in less than five minutes." Ask the right questions to learn what is missing, give people the opportunity to discover the right answers and then invite them to act.

Persuasion over Manipulation

When your customers have an agenda or point of view that is inconsistent with your own, it is less effective to state your point of view and hope your customer agrees. It is more effective to clarify their point of view first. Let them know that you are more focused on their needs than your wants. Once the customer's point of view is clear, your next objective is to demonstrate a sound understanding of their point of view as well as the points you have in common. Once you reach some common ground, and the customer feels understood, you can then begin asking questions that help the customer see your logic.

This is persuasion at work, take care not to be closed-minded of their answers. When your customer's answers continue to be inconsistent with your agenda, you have two options: 1) continue to ask questions that will help the customer see the matter in a different light; or 2) explore a third alternative with the customer that neither of you had explored previously. By following this method, you will be more persuasive, create more WOW Experiences and enjoy long-term customer relationships without resorting to short-term gains met through control or manipulation.

"Win/win is a belief in the third alternative. It's not your way or my way; it's a better way."

—Stephen R. Covey

Grandma Said, "If You Ask, You Don't Get"

Grandma Wilson had no idea the impression she left on me so many years ago as we sat down to watch British sitcoms late at night. This tradition at my grandparent's house became a tremendous learning experience. While my grandparents were laughing at crude jokes on TV, I would enjoy a nice bowl of ice cream or some M&Ms and sometimes I was fortunate enough to get the two mixed together. One night, my grandma forgot to give me a treat before turning on her show. So I asked her, "Hey grandma...no ice cream tonight?"

You should have seen the scowl on her face as she responded, "Brigham if you ask you don't get." Now, I couldn't help but notice that I seemed to be pushing her buttons. I didn't quite understand why, so I continued to press, "But Grandma, if I don't ask, how will you know that I want ice cream?"

After a long sigh, she put down the remote control, walked into the kitchen for a couple of minutes and came back out with a bowl of my favorite ice cream.

It turns out that *I* was right: *If you don't ask...you don't get.*

So, what do you want? If you're looking to create real value for your customer, ask for the sale early during the interaction and ask for it often. Who knows, your customer may take you up on it! And if they say "*no*," so what! You had nothing to lose in the first place—you only have something to gain by asking.

Self-Discovery

If the purpose of this human experience is to find fulfillment and improve our time while we are here, then it is important for us to become more aware of what will bring us happiness through self-discovery. This wasn't always important to me. Through experiencing my greatest adversity, losing practically everything I owned, I developed an inner need to make a difference. Where are you in the process of learning how to make a difference? Have you found your passion? That thing that literally rips you out of bed in the morning ready to start a new day?

There is so much meaning in life, and by asking yourself what is important to you and applying the Pattern for Excellence, you will have the ability to catapult yourself to a higher level in a fraction of the time. Steven R. Covey, the author of *The 7 Habits of Highly Effective People*, taught that happiness in life comes down to your relationships and accomplishments and that neither is achieved at a high level without having a value-driven purpose and the ability to communicate that purpose to others.

Assessment: When is the last time you asked yourself what was missing? What old habits do you need to break? What healthy habits do you need to develop?

It is a blessing to reside in a country with so many freedoms, opportunities, and privileges. What are you doing with that freedom? Where much is given, much is required.

Hopefully, your goals and aspirations in life are to contribute to the greater good. What will make you indispensable at home, in your business, and your community? Make it your watchword to find fulfillment in servicing others and creating WOW Experiences.

> *Watchword* "a word or phrase expressing a person's or group's core aim or belief."
>
> —*Google Free Dictionary*

In our coaching company, we train people to WOW more customers by asking the right questions that empower others to clarify what is missing and discover the right answers for themselves. Once they know what they should do, we simply invite them to do it. Since happiness in this human experience is found in the service of others, we all need to lose ourselves in purposeful work and create as many WOW Experiences as possible.

Ask and You Shall Receive

From the time I was a kid, I wrote letters to Santa asking for the coolest toys of the year. Did you do that? During Halloween did you say, "Trick or treat!" to get candy? If you wanted a treat before dinner, you had to ask for it. Right? Even later in life, when you wanted to date that girl or guy of your dreams—you had to *ask*. When you got that job, you had to *ask*. And, if you have kids, you probably teach them that if they want something, they have to *ask*. No matter the situation, *if you want something, you have to ask.*

We all grew up with the *Ask* principle and didn't even know it. This principle applies to a myriad of situations, including business. If you want your call handling team to book more calls and keep your field staff in the field where they belong, you need to make sure they are asking for that appointment. If they don't ask, *they don't get, and neither do you.*

During the first part of my coaching and consulting program, my team listens and monitors how the client's calls are handled. My team notes that many call handlers in the training and coaching program never ask to book an appointment. It is similar to walking into a business that begins their monolog explaining who they are and what they do, only to finish it with something like "That's us! If you would like any of our products or services, just let us know."

They seem to have answered the customer's initial questions, shared what they do, but haven't capitalized on the opportunity by *asking for the business.* Merely letting the customer know what you do and that you *can* help does not equate to *actually helping* by asking them for the opportunity. Companies wonder why and even act surprised when they have a low volume of booked calls! I tell them that all of the expense and effort that go into advertising and staffing is worthless if their call handling team is not asking for the appointment.

To increase your number of booked calls dramatically, teach your call handling team to ask for the appointment at the beginning of the call. A potential customer is calling you because they have a problem. As soon as your call handling team understands the situation and affirms they can help, they need to ask when the customer would like a field staff employee to come out to their home. *"When would you like us to come out?"* It's that easy.

Now, do the math. If your call handling team only books *one more call a day* because of this tip, how much would that equal in one year? If your average ticket is $200 and you book just one more call per day, that equals an extra $52,000 a year in your pocket— and that doesn't include weekends! $52,000 in revenue (or more) a year and it doesn't cost you a thing!

If you don't ask, you don't get. To create more WOW Experiences, ask the right questions to help your clients consider the right answers. As soon as your customers settle in on the desired outcome, invite them to respond accordingly. Listen and discern what is missing, discover the right answers and respond accordingly.

Write down what you know to be true about this principle. Consider personal experiences or stories you have heard that confirm your belief in the *Ask* principle. Articulate a game plan to put what you know and believe into action. Do it enough times and that action becomes a habit.

10 Principle 7: Be Valuable Inspire Conscious Creation

We create value within the responsibility we are given and coach others to do as we are doing

Pre-assessment question: Are you giving customers what they ask for or what they want?

By creating value within the responsibility we are given and by coaching others to do as we are doing, the value is multiplied. I recently had the extreme pleasure of experiencing this in real time with my six-tear-old, Isaac. At the drive-thru at Chick-Fil-A, there was a lady standing outside with a headset taking orders. I asked for my usual meal and topped it off with their yummy lemonade. After I had ordered, Isaac told me he wanted root beer. Why Isaac wanted root beer was beyond me. We *always* ordered lemonade. He even tried to convince me on our way up to the window that he *always* orders root beer. Now I knew that wasn't true, but I still felt bad that I hadn't been able to order him his drink.

We pulled up to the window and watched as another lady with a headset prepared our order. Isaac wore a pitiful frown, and I told him that next time I would get him a root beer. The lady with our order popped her head out and said politely, "Brigham, here is some root beer for your son." How did she know my name or that my son wanted root beer? As I sat there somewhat bewildered, I handed the root beer to Isaac, who immediately perked up and smiled wide. When I expressed my gratitude, she replied "My pleasure." I sat back in my chair. My pleasure? How often do we get that sentiment?!

It took me a half a mile to figure out what happened. The first lady with a headset standing out by the drive-through took my name before taking my order. The second lady in the window used my name when giving me the root beer for Isaac. She knew he wanted root beer because she watched me promise him that next time he could get a root beer. She took a risk and gave me root beer to cheer up my son. If that wasn't enough to WOW me, when I expressed my appreciation, she said, "My pleasure."

If she had given me what I ordered, my expectation would have been met. It's not her fault that I ordered my son lemonade. I was comfortable taking full responsibility for getting him a drink he didn't want. Instead, she anticipated my need and provided what Isaac *really* wanted and created a memorable experience that I have shared many a time when giving examples of WOW Experiences.

She took a risk even though the gesture could have backfired, especially if I did not want Isaac to have root beer. She went for it, and it paid off. She created a WOW Experience.

Give Others What They Really Want

Anyone can deliver what was is ordered. To give others what they *really* want requires our best effort to discover what they need and deliver value beyond what they expected. Don't just give people what they ordered, give them what they want!

How do professional athletes serve and deliver value? People want to watch their athletic team and are willing to pay top dollar. Athletes provide a service that entertains, and we pay for the experience. We all serve in different ways and deliver a different product but in the end, we are all still serving. What about actors? Actors can't make a living unless people want to see them act. They serve by acting to the best of their ability and creating value when you go to the movie theater. The same holds true with every other profession. Serving is providing something of value to others. What if athletes and actors only did what was expected? No WOW would be experienced. Would you be willing to pay to go to a football game or watch an actor if they never surprised you but only gave you what you expected or received last time?

You create WOW Experiences when the value you create exceeds the investment of time and money made by your customer. In other words, you do something unexpected. You exceed or modify expectations. To outwork means to "work harder, faster, better or longer than." Confidence comes because you have outworked the competition. Your income is a byproduct of the value you bring to the table. The individuals and companies that create the most value for their customers are the ones who succeed.

Creating value comes down to thinking about *why* you do what you do. Not just the practice but the principle and purpose behind what you do. Once you find the *why* behind the *what* it becomes easier, almost effortless, to create value for others in unique and innovative ways.

For example, my experience at Chick-Fil-A would have been much different if there was no one standing next to the drive-thru to take my name. I could have just as easily talked to a faceless box with an intercom in front of a life-size menu. I also could have paid at one window and picked up my order out of the next like they do at any other fast-food restaurant.

Why did they go to so much trouble at Chick-Fil-A? They went out of their way to serve me. They created value within the responsibility they were given. They didn't just give me what I ordered; they gave me what I *really* wanted. They WOWed me.

Chick-Fil-A brings in more money per location on average than McDonald's, and they are not open on Sundays. Yes, their chicken sandwiches are great, but let's face it, the experience they create far outweighs the taste of their food. By the way, when you go into a

Chick-Fil-A, it is customary for employees to come over to your table and ask to refill your drink or offer you additional service. How's that for a fast-food restaurant?!

Build Your Brand with Great Service

Suppose that you own a company in the Residential Home Service Industry. Undoubtedly, your technicians (techs) are a vital part of your service business. You train them continuously because they're on-site, doing everything from troubleshooting to repairs and upselling. But before your highly trained techs even get a chance to show off their skills, you have another team who is responsible for booking the calls that get the techs in front of the customer, your customer service reps (CSRs) on your call handling team.

Your CSRs are on the front lines—the first voice new customers hear when they call into your business—and their ability to WOW your customers will set the stage for the tech to show off their training and expertise. Knowing this, you might ask yourself: Compared to your techs, how much training do you give your CSRs? How often are you evaluating their performance and working with them to improve their skills? If you're not regularly training or working with them to improve their skill sets, why not?

Thanks to top-selling *experience*-driven companies like Zappos and Chick-Fil-A, customers have come to expect great service at every level. CSRs may not seem as important as techs because they do not meet the customer face-to-face, but they deliver the crucial first impression with every person who calls in for service.

As the saying goes, *"You never get a second chance to make a first impression,"* and the interaction your CSRs have with customers leaves a lasting impression that reflects your brand, for better or worse. So, why not make those interactions better—or, better yet, phenomenal? Training your CSRs to WOW customers can transform a call into a sale and information-seekers into long-term clients.

Imagine the impact this would have on your brand, potentially creating not just clients, but *raving fans*!

Your CSRs need continued training similar to techs so they can practice creating WOW Experiences for your customers. Consider the current state of your brand in every customer interaction, whether over the phone, in the customer's home, at your office or on the showroom floor. What steps can you take to create value in every interaction?

Putting Your Purpose into Your Practice

Last year I had the pleasure of working with Butcher Distributing. They wanted to help their warehouse and front-counter employees create value within the responsibility given, and wow experiences for their contractors.

On the surface, some would think that there's not much to their job. Contractors need parts to fix and install heating and cooling systems in the customer's home. Butcher Distributing would ensure the contractor had the right parts and systems on their trucks so that they could install and fix homeowners heating and air conditioning. Pretty simple, right?

What happens when a contractor gets to the home of one of their customers, and they don't have the right parts? The contractor has to go back to the distributor and get the right parts. They look unprepared and maybe even incompetent in front of the homeowner, not to mention the lost time and money it takes to go back and forth. It's a quick way to lose a client.

"Accuracy First" happens to be Butcher Distributing's company purpose. The general manager at Butcher didn't want their company purpose to just hang on the wall—he wanted it to be a living and breathing part of his company.

I explained what some of the best in customer service companies such as Zappos, Southwest, and Chick-Fil-A were doing and the value they were creating for their customers. Butcher employees began coming up with their own ideas on how to create WOW Experiences in their customer interactions. They saw that they could create that WOW by infusing their company purpose into everything they did. They focused on each customer interaction starting with the phone. The greeting before was generic, at best: *"Thank you for calling Butcher."* Other times it was just *"Butcher,"* followed by an eerie pause, waiting for the contractor to speak, which is fine because that was the same level of service that the contractor received from other distributors.

During my time at Butcher, they created a greeting that was uniquely their own: *"Fast is fine, but Accuracy is First, this is (Name), how may I help you."* The greeting is positive for sure, and it also reinforces their purpose. It reminds the contractor and the employee what they are all about every time they get on the phone. During the call, they would ask the contractor if it would be alright to check the order for accuracy. They would list the items on the contractor's order, along with other necessary items and parts the contractor might need but did not include in the order. At the end of the call, the Butcher employee would ask the contractor how they liked the service and if everything in the order was accurate.

Before my time with Butcher, the experience was much like any other distributorship. So, during the training, we also revamped the way they interact with customers in person. When contractors walk through the front door of their service center, a doorbell rings to let the employees at the front counter know that a customer has arrived. Originally, they wouldn't say anything to the contractor other than a forced *"hello"*, but now they say in unison, *"Welcome to Butcher, we are trained to help you."*

Now, when a contractor comes to the front counter with an order, the warehouse employee comes to the front counter to retrieve the order and starts loading the product and parts into the contractor's truck. Once the ordered product and parts are loaded, the warehouse employee asks permission to check the order with the contractor to ensure everything on the list is in the truck. The warehouse employee suggests other parts that the contractor might need during the home installation to avoid a second trip back to Butcher.

The warehouse employee and the contractor then walk back to the front counter, in front of the warehouse employee, the front counter employee asks the contractor if the order has been checked for accuracy. He makes one last check to ensure the contractor has everything that is needed to complete the job in the customer's home. Similar to the end of a phone call at Butcher, they ask the contractor, *"How was our service today? Was everything accurate?"*

Moreover, a bell is mounted on the wall next to the front counter, and above the bell, a sign reads: *"Ring this bell if you liked our service."* When the bell rings, Butcher employees that hear it all shout in unison, *"accuracy first."*

You might wonder if there are unnecessary redundancies in their performance, or even if the "scripted" greetings and questions make them sound robotic. First of all, in the home service business, time is money. If you have to go back to get parts, you can kill profitability. Secondly, a "scripted" response is a launching pad to WOW Experiences and is meant to reflect what the company believes in, not what the employees are forced to say. When companies and their employees share in the company vision, such statements as *"Welcome to Butcher, we are trained to help you"* do not come off as insincere or scripted, but rather as passionate declarations of true altruism. In the end, it is better to make sure the company gets it right the first time, and that everyone there believes in the company vision. Butcher does just that, creating a WOW Experience that keeps contractors coming back for more.

Build Value by Being Capable and Creative

I tell my kids that if a job is worth doing, then it's worth doing right, usually because I don't agree with the way they cleaned their room or did the dishes. How hard can it be? Especially when you have free room and board?

Whatever you do, *do it well*. Do it better than anyone else. When you do, it makes you feel good, and your customers will come back for more because they respect your capability to deliver a consistent, quality product and service. To create WOW Experiences, you must first learn that no matter the endeavor, you need to be prepared to do well. Whether someone is watching or not, your best performance repeated over and over creates fulfillment at work and makes you indispensable to those you serve.

Consider these creative ways to build value:

- Chick-Fil-A employees walk by your table to make sure you're happy with your meal and refill your drink if needed.
- If your FitBit stops working for any reason, you'll get a new one with no questions asked, even if your dog ate it.
- At Buckey's, you can try all the jerky you'd like whether you buy or not. Good luck walking out of there without jerky though. It's awesome! If you have not been to a Buckey's on your way from Austin to Houston, it's time for a road trip. That's WOW!

This year, our coaching company launched a new training product. We go on site to set the expectation for phone interactions with customers. Once the training date is set, we immediately ship out a "WOW Box" with explicit instructions not to open the box until the trainer arrives. The box is full of five to eight kinds of promotional materials—such as mouse pads, stress balls, posters, pens, manuals, and shirts—to hand out during the training. It makes the training experience fun and memorable and sets the tone for ongoing coaching during the call handling certification process.

When you create value, you are providing a service unique to your client, and that is what will keep them coming back to you. If a job is worth doing, make sure you do it right. Use the Pattern for Excellence to uncover what your customers really want, not just what they ordered. Take a risk and create value within the responsibility you have been given to WOW more customers.

Independent of what you practice, you are serving. Why did the busboy at the Texas Roadhouse not just clean the table in a minute and then retreat into the kitchen but instead draw a heart with his white rag, kiss his hand, slap it on the table and take a bow? He figured out what he was really doing independent of his practice; he was serving me, and he was doing it in an innovate way that gave him a sense of pride and created an experience for the rest of us. His performance was gratifying because he freely gave a service that we did not pay for or expect. It was a *WOW Experience*! The unique value he created made him valuable—even invaluable. His boss could not pay him enough to equal the value he was creating. Are you invaluable to your organization?

Do You Consider Yourself Valuable?

Your aim is to become *indispensable* to your organization. How do you accomplish that aim? By being clear on what others want. You treat them the way *they* want to be treated intentionally and on purpose. Be innovative in your approach, even if that requires a little discomfort. Remember how fulfilling it is to create WOW Experiences for others. Your positive energy will soar as you create value for others. It will feel good.

You feel good as you go above and beyond to create WOW and help others feel good when interacting with you. These good vibes between you and the client are perpetuated. When you create value for clients independent of how hard it is, how long it takes or how much you are being compensated to provide it, you become invaluable. Be valuable by creating value within the responsibility you are given and teach others to do the same!

Take a minute and write down what you know to be true about this principle. Share a personal experience or story that reinforces your belief in this principle. Create an action plan that will turn what you know and believe about this principle into action. Repeated action becomes a habit.

11 Principle 8: Be Grateful
Honor Our Stewardship

*Serving others together in stewardship
is a blessing that we honor and value*

*Pre-assessment question: Do you consider your role as work or an
opportunity to service others?*

When you say *"Thank you,"* what you are communicating is *"You Matter"* or *"You've made a difference."* When people feel like they have made a difference, they feel important. When they feel important, their tendency is to become loyal to you and your company.

How many customers today are truly loyal? They are hard to come by, and so we ought to be grateful for every loyal customer we have. Gratitude builds loyalty!

How Can You Show Gratitude to a Client?

Remember, a WOW Experience is giving MORE than expected. It's about creating value within your responsibility. Something as simple as saying "Thank you" creates a sense of value. To make a "Thank You" WOW worthy, it has to be more than a polite gesture. We like to call it *"Thank You with Evidence."*

Of course, you first say "thank you," but then you back it up with *Why* you are thankful for the client and their business. For example, imagine that a repeat client calls in and has an issue with a previously repaired unit and needs additional service. Here is one way to show your gratitude *and* deliver some WOW.

(Client Calls In)

CSR: "It's a great day at ABC Heating and Cooling, this is Amanda. How can I make your day?"

Homeowner: "Amanda, this is Sue Powers. You folks have been to my home before. I have another issue with my furnace again. I should have had you guys replace it the last time you were here."

CSR: "Yes Sue, I see that we have serviced your furnace a couple of times now. I am so saddened to hear that your furnace is not working again."

Homeowner: "Oh, that's alright. I am just happy to have you guys around to help me!"

CSR: "Sue, that means a lot to us; in fact, I would like to thank you for contacting us again. In this competitive industry, having clients return to us for service is key to our success. I want to let you know that we do not take that for granted. We are VERY grateful.

               "And because you have been so good to us, I want to share something with you. By looking at your account, I can see that you are not a member of our Customer Service Club that gives special savings to loyal clients like you. Do you know about our club?"

Homeowner: "I think your technician Billy may have mentioned it to me last time he was here, but I don't remember."

CSR: "Well Sue, I bring this up because if you were a member, you would have already saved more than the cost of the membership. Plus, if your equipment eventually fails, as a member you get a portion, or potentially all, of your prior investment applied to replacing your equipment. It is ideal for someone like you. I hate to see a loyal client not enjoy the most savings possible. Would you like to take advantage of this and join our club?"

Homeowner: "It sounds like a great deal. Thank you so much for bringing that up!"

CSR: "Sue, that is the least I can do after all you have done for us by returning as a loyal customer! Let me just collect a little information, and we can get Billy back out there. Now that you're a member you'll never have to pay a dispatch fee again to have us come out!"

You build loyalty by being grateful. Some might question the validity of these examples or principles claiming them to be "cheesy" or "fake." I remind you that the scripts and examples provided are meant to be launching pads. The most well-versed and gifted of all salespeople won't be able to create WOW Experiences without being genuine. Altruism is key. To build loyalty you have to put the *task mindset* aside and focus on the goal; to create a WOW Experience for the customer and create value beyond the customer's expectation.

You do that by being positive, confident, listening, caring, saying "*Yes*," asking the right questions, creating unique value and being grateful. As you do, you are going to WOW more customers, and your business will grow as a result.

Example of a WOW *"Thank You"*

I have a good friend, Kean Farr, who is well into his 80's, but his mind is sharp. When I talk to Kean, the conversation is always deep because we talk about family, relationships, accomplishments, and life's purpose. He is highly intelligent and speaks from life experience, so it's always an insightful, thought-provoking conversation.

During one of these conversations, Kean was talking about the friends that he grew up with and how they were now beginning to pass away. He also hinted that he was not far behind them. My heart saddened at the thought, and I blurted out, "You CAN'T die!" He laughed initially at my comment but appreciated the sentiment. He then went on to explain the nature of things as they are and admitted that he had no choice in the matter. He would at some unknown point and time, pass away like everyone else. "Kean," I said, "you are the sage in the neighborhood. The rest of us here still have much to learn from you." To which he replied, "Oh, it's sage you want." And with a glimmer in his eye, he quickly changed the subject.

I noticed the abrupt switch but chalked it up to the fact that he was getting older, assuming he may have lost track of the topic of our conversation. Two days later, he showed up at my front door with some sage leaves in hand, "Here you are Brigham. After I'm gone, you'll still have 'Sage.' My work here is done." He then proceeded to give me some sage advice as we stood just inside my front door. He asked me if I remembered when my wife invited him to a youth campout about five years previous. Kean went to the campout and addressed the youth, which went great. Two weeks later he received a thank-you letter in the mail from my wife. She expressed her appreciation for him as well as the lasting positive impression he left on the youth who attended.

He then said, "Brigham, you might get a phone call or email where someone expresses some appreciation, but rarely today do you get a thank-you letter. I have to tell you that every time I see your wife to this day, I cannot help but think of her thank-you letter."

Now that is a WOW Experience! Why? When you express appreciation to someone, you are communicating that the person made a difference. When you help others feel they have made a difference through your expression of appreciation, they feel important. When people feel important, they become loyal to you and your company.

Loyalty means that your clients will stand by you, independent of what others say. They will even stick up for you, defend you, and become advocates for you. Gratitude is extremely powerful because it makes others more tolerant, amiable and patient with you, even when things don't go exactly as planned or there is a mistake.

Avoid phrases such as "no problem" or "you're welcome". These phrases do not show gratitude. Break the bad habit of using the phrase, "no problem." Since this common phrase has a double negative in it, "no" and "problem." Avoid using these two words. Saying "you're welcome" communicates that you are doing the customer a favor—not the other way around.

Remember, ultimately the customer who calls in or comes into your store pays the bills and keeps your company in business. So when you talk to a client, be grateful for their business. Regardless of the state they are in, express sincere appreciation. If the client beats you in saying, "thank you" at the end of your transaction, just respond by saying, "my pleasure."

Remember that in a WOW Experience the Giver benefits as much as, if not more, than the Receiver. Human beings are meant to serve and help one another. As Stephen R. Covey said, "Happiness is rooted in relationships and accomplishments." It is essential to do your work with a positive attitude and develop your confidence by achieving mastery in your profession—thus becoming the absolute best at what you do.

You improve your relationships and increase your accomplishments as you learn to excel in your ability to listen, care, say "Yes," and ask the right questions. Remember what Zig Ziglar said, "In order to get what you really want, you need to help others get what they want."

Once you know what they really want, you create value by giving it to them—not just what they first asked for or initially ordered. You then polish off the entire experience by expressing sincere gratitude. You tell them that they made a difference and that they are important, and that's how they become loyal to you.

The more you WOW people, the more successful your relationships become, your achievements increase and the happier you'll be. Serving others together in stewardship is a blessing that we honor and value and it is fulfilling.

The principles in the Pattern for Excellence are not new—they have been taught, in one way or another, since the beginning of time. The only difference is that you have a repeatable pattern you can use as you put them into practice. By implementing the Pattern for Excellence, you gain the mindset and communication skill set that you need to help others get what they want, develop rich and rewarding relationships and accomplish many wonderful things in your life.

You cannot achieve personal fulfillment by focusing on yourself. The opposite is true. What brings true joy is losing yourself in a purpose that is greater than you. Alcohol, drugs, high-risk adrenaline sports, fast cars, entertainment, money and all the rest bring only temporary thrills or momentary amusement. My friend Kean Farr, now near the end of his life experience, values none of these things. The only thing he talks about, the only thing that matters in the end to him, are his relationships and accomplishments.

Remember that in a WOW Experience, you are the Giver. The Pattern for Excellence is the process that keeps on giving. Givers must see the work they do as meaningful, bigger than themselves and be self-driven to provide WOW service without considering how hard it is, how long it takes, or how much they are being compensated. They provide high-level service because they believe in the cause, the Why.

Receivers always expect a good level of service. In a WOW interaction between Giver and the Receiver, both walk away edified because the Giver gives *amazing* and *unexpected* service freely. This relationship becomes reciprocal when the Receiver is so impressed by the Giver's service that he tells all his friends. The WOW Experience is the outcome we desire in every customer interaction; it makes us feel good and produces the results we want.

You have a decision to make. It's one that's easier said than done. You can no longer justify standing idly by and hope others around you will step up. Your clients' expectations are very high, and a *Pattern* has been outlined in great detail to follow and assist you in finding purpose in what you do—in every role in your life, whether it be at work, at home, or at play. This is your opportunity to find fulfillment by forgoing self and engaging in a work that is far greater than you.

Enjoy the WOW Journey

Remember that we must enjoy the journey—not just the destination—one WOW Experience at a time. If the job is worth doing, let's do it right! It requires self-mastery and sacrifice. But I can assure you from experience that once you master the principles in the Pattern for Excellence, you will WOW more customers, you will be the best at what you do, and you'll experience more success and fulfillment in your life.

Take a few minutes to write down what you know to be true about this principle. Consider personal experiences or stories you have heard that confirm your belief in the *Be Grateful* principle. Articulate a game plan to put what you know and believe into action. Do it enough times and that action becomes a habit.

SECTION 3

WOW
PERFORMANCE

How you create and sustain it

In this third section, we explore how to deliver WOW Service, create a WOW Culture, and sustain WOW Performance. At the end of the day, your service *performance* speaks louder to your customers than your service *promise.* Action speaks louder than words.

12 Delivering WOW Service

From Transactions to Transformational Relationships

C onsider a few of the hard times or difficult experiences you have had over the last decade—perhaps an illness, accident, trial, bankruptcy, divorce or death of a family member. Difficulties are part of the human experience. We all suffer setbacks and hope we'll never have to deal with similar circumstances again.

In your client interactions, you likely have no idea what the client may be going through; however, this is your opportunity to influence their state of being in a positive way. Your chances of having a favorable impact are greater when you apply the Master Principles in the Pattern for Excellence. By using the Pattern for Excellence, you will create more WOW Experiences and be the bright spot in someone's otherwise, "bad day."

Providing a positive customer service experience doesn't just make others feel good—it can be the *one* thing that separates your business from your competition. At a time when anyone can find the market price of your products or services with the click of a button, you need to find a way to differentiate yourself beyond cost or risk commoditization. Today, it is all about the customers' experience and how you make them feel. We have heard customers exclaim that despite the cost your company charges above the competition, they will keep coming back because they love the way the company makes them feel. The WOW Experience will create a loyal customer who not only returns to you for more service but tells all their friends too!

Use These 10 Master Keys

How can you consistently deliver WOW customer service experiences? You need keys to open the doors (and windows) of opportunity:

Key #1 - Uncover a cause that is bigger than yourself; an aim you are working toward or a fundamental reason for your organization's existence. Once it is evident and shared by you and your team, it will serve as powerful motivation. Knowing what you do is not enough—you should come to a belief of *why* you are doing it.

Key #2 - Be positive on purpose so that the passion for what you do is electric and contagious.

Key #3 - Be confident by choice, through continued practice and preparation. Remember, the magic happens because of the time and effort you have put into the mechanics.

Key #4 - Listen intentionally to connect on an emotional level and remain present to their expression, tone, and intent.

Key #5 - Actively invite others to connect and become present in the moment with you by genuinely expressing empathy and respect for their worth.

Key #6 - Deliberately give first, to create WOW Experiences and build long-term relationships.

Key #7 - Hold yourself accountable to clarify what is missing, discover the right answers and respond accordingly.

Key #8 - Proactively search out and act upon ways to create value within the responsibility you are given and encourage others to do as you are doing.

Key #9 - Be sincere towards others in your stewardship. Show them that you honor and value the opportunity to serve.

Key #10 - Have a written plan of action for incorporating your *Why* into everything that your team does; phone interaction, in the office, on the showroom floor or onsite and hold yourself and team accountable to that plan.

Beyond understanding the Pattern for Excellence, you must intentionally, actively, deliberately, purposely, proactively and sincerely apply it. To win the moment, you must ACT! Apply the Principles intentionally to change hearts, minds and moods inside as well as outside of your organization. As you do, the transactions you have between you, your team and your clients will be transformed into powerful, rewarding, long-lasting relationships.

Power of WOW to Change Moods

Have you ever had such an amazing WOW Experience that it changed your mood for the rest of the day? What if you could do that for each and every customer? Do you think they would want to do business with you again? Yes, of course, they would!

Driving my daughter Fe to Chick-Fil-A, we passed a big truck unloading several boxes of lemons. I never imagined that the lemonade at Chick-Fil-A is freshly squeezed, and so I had to ask the lady through the window if they really used fresh lemons. She said, "Yes, of course" while handing us the breakfast we ordered. "All of our lemonade is freshly squeezed. It's quite an ordeal. Would you like to try some?"

I was a bit hesitant to accept her offer because I had sampled their lemonade plenty of times and felt I would be taking advantage. Then I remembered the experience they endeavor to create and graciously accepted the free lemonade. When I said, "thank you," she responded, "My pleasure." I just love that response!

Let's examine the experience she created. First, she was upbeat in her disposition. She was super friendly and pleasant. She came across as intelligent and informed, to the point where I almost would have believed whatever she said. She listened to my question and was sincere during our interaction. Her response was brilliant as she explained that it was quite an ordeal to produce the lemonade. Her offer to try some was above and beyond what I expected. I love Chick-Fil-A!

Do you see the Pattern for Excellence coming out in her interaction with me? Was she positive? Was she confident? Did she listen and care? Did she say, *"Yes?"* Did she ask the right questions? Did she create unique value for me based on my question? Was she grateful? On all accounts, yes! What was most impressive to me was how she created value as she explained the "ordeal" of making lemonade before asking me if I wanted to try some. She won the moment and made my day.

Why wouldn't you want to make someone's day? Remember that when you serve others and create value for them, you experience self-fulfillment. Losing yourself in the service of others creates a positive feeling for you, and helps your company see additional value in you. You become indispensable.

Wow Performance: Beyond Scripts and Sales Systems

Scripts and selling systems are used in nearly every call center and on every showroom floor. These scripts and systems help create a uniform voice for your business, serve as a set of useful guidelines for customer interactions, maintain focus and ensure that your call handlers and sales team know what to say. But what happens when the script or selling system doesn't work? Do you know when to *ditch the script or throw out the system*, and more importantly, how to create a WOW Experience with or without the script or system?

Customers will come to you with a myriad of different circumstances and expectations, and not every interaction will have a clear-cut, step-by-step progression that ends positively 100% of the time. *Being too dependent on a script or selling system can cause your team to lose out on the opportunity to work autonomously and custom build value into the product or service you provide.*

Scripts are a great starting point, but WOW service happens when your team learns to listen actively to and engage customers. To keep your conversions high, your team must feel empowered to go beyond the script or system when necessary to create a WOW Experience. Your team must be proactive and be able to create value for others of their free will, not because the script tells them to. When you apply the Pattern for Excellence, the knowledge and freedom to act independently allows your team to create more WOW Experiences. Be sure to give them the freedom to improvise when necessary by instructing them how to apply the principles in the Pattern—not just the script or selling system.

From Ordinary to Extraordinary: Motives and Mindset

Some organizations deliver poor service. Even with a great product, they struggle to keep customers. Many organizations provide ordinary service—just enough to keep their most loyal customers— as long as the product meets their needs. Few organizations deliver *exceptional service*—the kind that will WOW clients and keeps them coming back.

Every organization needs to **reverse** their **poor** and **ordinary** customer service performance to thrive. **Extraordinary** customer service is the new norm! So, how do you bring about a **reversal** in your service performance?

Wrestling Reversals: I wrestled in high school, and I am still trying to master "reversals" on the mat as well as in life. In wrestling, a "reversal" occurs when the wrestler on the bottom manages to reverse his position and come out on top of his opponent.

Service Reversals: I have interacted with many service managers and owners who desperately need to reverse their poor or ordinary service performance but have succumbed to the darker side of their **motives** and **methods** to improve service. They focus on profits over people, on practices over purposes, and on programs over principles.

When I address the need to WOW your customers, I start by talking about *motives* and *mindset* (then methods and skill set). Excellent customer service is not just something you *do*—it is a way of thinking. It is a state of *being*. In other words, it is both *motive* and *method, mindset* and *skill set*.

It takes time, practice, and a conscious effort to reverse a bad habit. Mastery of the principles in the Pattern for Excellence begins with *Why* over *What* or *How*. Commit your time and energy to cultivate a purpose driven state of mind, not just a skill set.

WOW Service Wins and Keeps Clients

Let me ask you two seemingly unrelated questions: 1) can you remember the last time a customer told you that they chose your company, independent of price because they'd been WOWed by you? 2) can you imagine adding an extra $100,000 a year to your bottom line (net profit) without having to spend more money on marketing or advertising?

Well, it can happen! If you or a member of your call handling team creates one more opportunity out of 20 incoming calls a day, and if your average ticket is $500, over a 250-day period your revenue will increase by at least $125,000 a year!

Yes, your company could *double* its revenue in two-to-five years, just by changing the way you handle incoming phone calls. When you are interacting with customers and potential customers, WOW service performance is the fastest, easiest way to make more money—and the clearest path to becoming indispensable to your organization!

Make Way for Market Transparency

The internet has leveled the playing field for businesses. Search engines like Google have empowered customers with full knowledge about your company and your competition. By enabling people to go online and see how much you and your competitors charge for a product or service, your product (or service) has slowly become commoditized.

Sites like **Yelp** and **HomeAdvisor** have become go-to venues for customers to share immediately and receive feedback on you and your competitors. The higher your service rankings, the better your chances that people will call you first.

Consequently, when customers call, they're expecting more than just, "Let me check the schedule." They're informed, and they will shop around if the first call doesn't meet their needs.

What does this mean for business owners and managers? As a business owner, you must equip yourself and your team with the tools necessary to deliver a more than average experience. Today, *you either WOW your customers or risk losing them to a better company*.

Most customers have two questions: 1) how soon can you get it done? 2) how much will it cost? Sure, customers want a good price, high quality, and convenience, but at the end of the day, customers buy *emotionally*. They need to like you and the service you provide. Beneath their immediate need to repair the broken air conditioner or unclog the toilet, for example, there's also an *emotional need* to know that you understand their angst and that you care *and* can help solve their problem.

Customers whose emotional need is fulfilled on their first call do not continue to shop around. They do not want to spend their entire day getting bids. They get bids because they feel the need to ensure they get a fair price. However, if you can show them you are the right company by the way you treat them during the call, you can convince them that they've called the right place and have no need to look further. You will have shown them using the Pattern for Excellence, that they have called the right company.

Go from Transaction to Connection to Transformation

Great service changes the *transaction* from a one-time exchange to a long-term *relationship* of repeat business. This *transformation* has the power to triple or even 10X the size and revenue of your business. Thus, your goal isn't just to *transact*; it's to *connect* and eventually *transform* the relationship.

Realizing this lofty goal requires "soft skills." So-called "soft skills" (people skills) may seem *soft*, but when customers experience them, the results are amazing because *soft* skills yield *hard* results! Yes, getting just one extra call a day can dramatically impact your company's bottom line. But without a tool that makes *excellence* an ingrained *pattern*, increased call success won't be consistent or repeatable.

Repetition is key—it doesn't happen overnight. The principles in the Pattern for Excellence must be taught again and again. Once you and your team understand what is expected, follow up with regularly scheduled progress meetings and practice or role-play different scenarios to maximize fresh opportunities.

Those in our ongoing coaching certification program are held accountable for the principles taught in the Pattern for Excellence, and the result is a transformation into customer service experts. Not only will they get those extra bookings, but they also WOW more customers by focusing on connections—not transactions.

Creating connections with customers goes beyond transaction— and it differentiates your business and improves your bottom line. When you positively engage with the customer and show that your company is listening and that you care, your customer finds it easy to say *"Yes"* to your services. People want to do business with you because you're connecting with them. When you make a connection, they feel that you understand their problem and you make their decision process easy.

Well-trained teams can connect with customers in four ways:

1) Actively listening to the customer first
2) Showing the customer that they care
3) Saying "Yes" to reassure the customer that they can help
4) Moving forward with the opportunity by learning what is missing and responding accordingly based on the desired outcome.

Customers want to be heard! They want to know that someone cares about their problem and is not just trying to sell them something. For example, one of my clients even turned a wrong number into a booked appointment by engaging the customer. Before the customer could hang up after realizing she had the wrong number, the handler asked, "Are you sure you don't need any plumbing or electrical services right now?"

The caller laughed at the question and then stopped in her tracks. "Actually," she said, "I do." The handler then asked for more information and moved forward by booking a time for her techs to stop by and take a look.

The call handler didn't just say, "Oh, sorry, you called the wrong number," and hang up. Instead, she was able to book a service call because she was trained to respond autonomously and connect with the caller. You see, more business is a byproduct of the WOW Experience you create! Your priority should be people over profits. Create more WOW to make more money.

WOW Experiences Exceed Expectations

When a customer experiences WOW, you are exceeding their expectations. You are addressing their needs thoughtfully and in unexpected ways. It is an expression of your authentic interest in the person who seeks your services, not just in the transaction or compensation. It is about making enduring personal and emotional connections with empathy, generosity, and gratitude. It is about awareness of common human concerns that make a difference. It is about truth, about meaning, and about details that cannot be measured by KPIs. In today's ultra-competitive markets, enduring businesses call for enduring relationships.

What do I mean when I refer to a "WOW" service? They are experiences—those unique, emotionally engaging interactions that go beyond the customer's expectation. As a service provider, that is your end goal. WOW service is different from good service. Those services that are considered "good" are expected. Those that are considered WOW Experiences, are unexpected.

I have a friend who consults on a multi-year customer experience project with Bob Yarmuth, CEO of the Sonny's Bar-B-Q Restaurant Franchise, the preeminent southern bar-b-q restaurant chain founded in Florida. Recently, he relayed to me a simple but "wow-full" service experience delivered by Christie Schatz, Director of HR for Sonny's. Christie was perusing customer communications when she ran across an email from a loyal customer, Buddy, who had recently moved into an area of Texas that did not have a Sonny's restaurant.

In the email, the customer asked if Sonny's planned to expand into his community. Christie responded, "Although we have no plans in place at this time to expand into your area, you can order Sonny's Bar-B-Q sauce online and have it shipped to you."

Christie's response represented good service. As a senior leader she was involved, responsive, direct, informative and helpful. Her timely communication clearly met the expectations of most people. But here's where the WOW comes in. After she had sent the email, Christie felt that she could easily do more, so she called the customer, confirmed his mailing address, and let him know that she would be sending Sonny's sauce to him! That is WOW!

People who have a difficult time understanding the value of "WOW" might wonder, "Why would she do that?" The man can't even frequent Sonny's stores if there none in his area. Or, perhaps the skeptics would raise a scalability or fairness issue, "Since you can't send sauce to everybody, why do it for this one guy?"

In essence, Christie cost-effectively did what was right for this engaged customer in that moment. The byproduct of that relatively small act of caring certainly got Buddy's attention; thus, he mentioned it on his blog, which turned into a podcast and a short YouTube video.

The customer, Buddy, has since repeatedly expressed gratitude and will likely share his WOW story with individuals who live near Sonny's franchises. And, I suspect that more customers will be inclined to buy sauce online and advocate on behalf of the brand. Remember, you give first to create WOW Experiences and build long-term relationships.

Start with the WOW in Mind

A WOW Experience is the single outcome we look to achieve in every customer interaction. Earlier I described the two roles in creating a WOW Experience: "Giver" and "Receiver."

The Giver must see the work they do as meaningful. They must believe it's bigger than themselves, and be self-driven to provide service without considering how hard the work is or how long it takes or how much they are compensated.

The Receiver has an expectation as to the kind of service they desire. In the interaction between the Giver and the Receiver, both walk away edified because the Giver provided a service that exceeded the expectations of the Receiver. That is the WOW Experience defined and is the outcome you should work toward in every customer interaction.

Excellent customer service is not just something you do—it is a state of being because it is both a mindset and a skill set. How do you naturally provide excellent service and how do you instill that mindset into your organization? Viewing your work as a set of tasks impedes progress while autonomous work magnifies progress hundred-fold.

What is the result of those who work together autonomously in a cause far greater than themselves? Here is the best analogy for this concept: Only 5% of the world's population resides in the United States, yet more new wealth has been created here than in the rest of the world combined. We went from horse and buggy to sending a man to the moon in less than two centuries. How did we as a nation accomplish this?

Think of Thomas Edison's light bulb, Alexander Bell's telephone, and the Wright brothers' airplane. What allowed them to create ingenious inventions and our country to move forward more quickly than any other nation? How about Steve Jobs, Jeff Bezos, S. Truett Cathy, et al? Our free republic has provided an environment that encourages autonomous thinking and applauds noble causes. Certainly, there have been others with equal opportunity, but only those with a strong belief and a purpose that propelled them forward achieved such greatness. We are and will continue to be the cumulative result of many great causes as long as we continue to remain free to fail, free to succeed or die trying.

The Power of Selling an Experience

When you think about an amazing experience with a business, what's the first company that comes to mind? Perhaps it is Amazon, Disney, Chick-fil-A, Southwest Airlines or Zappos. Whatever company pops into your head, chances are they came to mind first because they provided you with an amazing, unique experience— one that you will never forget.

Once you have an unexpected experience, the next time you come to expect it. So the question then becomes: Why aren't you doing that for your customers? Or more importantly: Why didn't your own business come to mind first?

If you are the owner of a company, growing your business is always at the forefront of your mind. Making the phone ring or getting customers into your store is often the first thing you consider when targeting growth. But if you're not making the most out of every customer interaction, you could be missing a valuable opportunity to grow your business, without spending an extra dime on advertising or marketing.

Meet Tony Hsieh

In 2003, Tony Hsieh (pronounced shay) founder of Zappos, decided to drop his advertising budget and shift his focus from advertising to great customer service. Within 12 months of taking that risk, he went from $70 million to $180 million in annual revenues. Today, Zappos customer service is so good that 75% of their orders come from repeat customers!

> *"Our whole philosophy became 'let's take most of the money we would've spent on paid advertising and paid marketing and instead invest it in the customer experience and then let our customers do the marketing for us through word of mouth' and that became the whole business model."*
>
> —Tony Hsieh, CEO, Zappos

What Are You Really Selling?

The first step to offering a unique experience is to find your purpose. Your purpose doesn't have to be what you sell; usually, your purpose is something greater than what you sell.

Zappos' purpose is not to sell shoes but to "deliver happiness and create a WOW Experience for every client." Southwest Airlines' purpose is not "To fly you places," but instead "To connect people to what's important in their lives through friendly, reliable, and low-cost air travel." Chick-Fil-A has a purpose: "To glorify God by being a faithful steward of all that is entrusted to them and have a positive influence on all who come in contact with Chick-Fil-A."

Success leaves clues. What is your purpose? What drives you? What makes you get up in the morning and go to work? Do you work for the money, recognition or to solve a problem and make people's lives easier—if it's the later, that's your purpose. Dedicate considerable time brainstorming and creating your company's purpose. In a short, memorable phrase, capture what is unique about your business and how the customer benefits from your uniqueness. Think about what drives you, your employees, and your customers to be excited about what you do and how you do it. Cultivate the mindset, not just the skill set.

Put Your Purpose into the Customer's Experience

Once you identify your purpose, look for ways to infuse it into every customer interaction and create an amazing experience that motivates clients to return for more WOW Experiences.

Every customer touchpoint is an opportunity to create a unique experience—one that will set you apart from your competition as well as reinforce your purpose. Teaching employees to represent your purpose in creative ways during their interaction reminds them of the "*Why*" in their actions.

You can include your company's purpose during the customer conversation and sales process, and again when you book an appointment or close the sale. You can even use it in your greeting. For example, consider which greeting sounds better: "XYZ Mechanical, this is Mike," or "XYZ keeps your home cozy and comfortable. This is Mike; how may I help you?"

Simply by changing your greeting, you improve your customer's experience and reinforce your company brand or main reason why customers should choose you. Immediately you create an elevated customer experience which sets you above the competition.

Weaving your purpose into each interaction in your organization not only improves your customer's experience, but it also creates loyal customers. You get customer reviews online that speak to how great you are and reinforce the brand you are building. Your customers stop caring about how much something costs because the positive experience you create is so different, so unique, that they buy your product regardless of the price.

Customers know when they experience something great. A personal connection, going the extra mile, and being the solution, all help create a unique experience that customers remember—and it all revolves around your purpose. When you discover your purpose, coming to work will become much more fun and exciting—both for you and your team. And, providing a unique experience will leave your customers saying, "WOW, I want more!"

Age of the Customer

This is the age of the customer; and in this era of high consumer expectations, you need to focus on delivering exceptional, personalized customer experiences. Since it's getting harder to attract customers' attention and close sales, you need to create your own customer experience strategy for growing profitable revenue, connecting better with customers, and winning against serious competition. Since companies now compete mostly on the basis of customer experience, more consumer product investments are directed to customer experience innovations. Emerging technology is playing a bigger role in profitability and the customers' digital experiences.

Companies are renewing their focus on user experience—across channels, not just on one platform—as they try to differentiate themselves through customer experience. Creativity and innovation are key elements that companies employ to build brilliant customer experiences. Smart companies see the link between customer experience and business results. Indeed, the customer experience is a competitive differentiator, and ease of interaction is a key element of a quality customer experience.

Automation often kills the customer's experience. In one way or another, we've all experienced an automated attendant; in fact, now we've come to expect the robotic, "Press one for ..." They're just a part of the routine—another hurdle to jump through before we can get to the reason why we called in the first place. Automated attendants were designed to bring speed and improve call handling efficiency but they test the patience of your clients. With the growth experienced in many companies, automated attendants in some industries have become an unfortunate necessity—one that if removed, may cripple some inbound call centers.

How can your company remain focused on delivering a great customer experience if every customer has to go through a menu system before they can speak to a live person? If a customer calls your company, they want to talk to a human being and gain assurance that they have called the right place. If an automated attendant is the first thing a customer hears and they have an urgent issue, they will become annoyed and frustrated before your call handling team ever gets a chance to WOW them.

Hence, the person taking the call needs to know how to engage the customer with positivity and reassure them that their situation will be resolved. By consistently working with your team to create a WOW Experience every time a customer calls, you empower them to put the customer at ease and remove any negative effect an automated attendant may have produced. From there, your call handler can concentrate on getting the customer's issue resolved and gaining their trust.

Break the Commoditization Barrier

Since the Internet has commoditized most businesses to the point where your products and services can be procured just about anywhere, I suggest that you focus on the two guaranteed ways to win and keep business without competing on price: 1) product or service innovation beyond what the market expects; or 2) create new ways to provide excellent customer service! By consciously deciding to offer your customers, at no additional cost, the gift of a great experience over the phone or in person, you create brand loyalty that is not easily influenced by price. To grow your customer base, you must give them a reason not only to choose you but also to use you exclusively.

Remember that people buy emotionally. With a little innovation in your customer experience, you can offer the same product as your competition, but customers will choose you, even when the cost is higher. That's the power of innovation and great customer service! These are WOW Experiences in action, and it is the best thing you can do to differentiate yourself and rise above price wars.

13 Creating a WOW Culture

Ensure your customer has a WOW Experience

"Our number one priority is company culture. Our whole belief is that if you get the culture right, most of the other stuff like delivering great customer service or building a long-term enduring brand will just happen naturally on its own."

—Tony Hsieh, CEO, Zappos

Pre-assessment question: If you were to assess your company's culture, how strong would it be?

To consistently create WOW Experiences, you must establish a company *culture*. Strong and unique company culture will not happen on its own, it requires you to be purposeful. Why do you need a strong company culture? Because WOW Customer Experiences are about meaningful details. They are unique gestures, not part of a mechanical, scripted process—not born out of rules or "best practices." They are expressions of your company's culture, its shared values, and ideals that guide the employee's decisions and create exceptional outcomes.

How can you embed these culture factors into your products and services? When delivering a *WOW Experience*, the number-one challenge is for every player on your team to be autonomously engaged in a cause bigger than themselves, creating value and living by your company vision, day in and day out. Team members must be proactive in carrying out your vision within their responsibilities. The whole team, collectively, must be aligned in their approach. Otherwise, your company's vision can be derailed by urgency or the litany of repetitive tasks.

Our service performance is exposed through customer experience, whether excellent or lacking. The only way to deliver true WOW continuously is through *constant evolution*; adapting quickly to peoples' changing needs and fine-tuning what's most useful to your customers. It sometimes requires a slight course correction and other times, when you are off course, the correction may be enormous. You can no longer afford only to work *in* your business—you must also work *on* your business; establish its vision and maintain and strengthen a positive company culture.

Leaders Inspire/Instill: Wax On, Wax Off

How do you naturally provide great service and how do you *inspire and instill* (not *inspect* or *install*) that mindset into every member of your organization?

Ongoing training and accountability. By consistently working on your ability to connect with customers, positive interactions can become a common thread in your culture, and you and your team will turn even the toughest leads into selling opportunities.

Remember the movie *The Karate Kid* and that moment when you realize that "wax on/wax off" was more than an annoying way to get chores done? By practicing this unusual method, the young boy being mentored by the Sensei was actually learning karate!

Similar "muscle memory" can be formed by you and your team with regular, ongoing training and accountability. Even when the most difficult customers come your way, you are ready to provide the same WOW Experience as you would in a less challenging customer interaction. All it takes is the willingness to work toward perfecting the mechanics behind the "magic" you create.

Each client is different. Even though many customers may have similar situations and come to you because of the same problem, each has their own behavior style, personality, and background. As a result, you must treat them differently based on their individual needs. That's why mastering the principles found in the Pattern for Excellence is more powerful than following a system or script. When you use the Pattern for Excellence, you can proactively respond in a positive way to anything a customer says or does, regardless of *how* they say it.

The last thing you want is to hesitate or not know how to respond to a customer. Often, this occurs when a script or system you have memorized does not account for the unique need of the customer. Make sure you have the right training and accountability practices in place to develop the muscle memory so you can easily adapt and apply the principles found in the Pattern for Excellence. By doing so, you will be ready—no matter the circumstance.

It takes a lot of time and practice before you can respond in a natural way, but by repetitious practice and ongoing training, a strong culture of *consistency* is developed that will improve customer service and boost productivity.

You Can Become Indispensable

Yes, **independent of the role you play at work, you can become indispensable.** Some company positions often get a bad rap. Individually, many call center agents feel as if they are at the bottom of the totem pole with no way to move up, and often they are treated in a way that perpetuates that feeling. Some may also have responsibilities in other areas of the company; as money collectors, administrative assistants or office managers, making it an even more demanding job, frequently with little appreciation or reward.

In reality, every position filled by a talented and willing human being plays a vital role in the success of a company. For example, the people who answer your phones represent the first impression your customer receives. If your "front line" feels devalued, burned-out or bored, your clients can't help but experience some of that in their interaction with your call handlers.

When you give your team ongoing training opportunities that teach them a marketable skill, it can awaken their passion for service and create a fresh career path. Employee-partners will begin to see their work as something greater than themselves—something they can embrace and take pride in.

Motivated call handlers can positively impact a company's bottom line through more booked calls, increased service agreement sales and more loyal customers. When regularly trained and rewarded for their work—perhaps through bonuses, commissions, awards, prizes or recognition—call handlers become empowered and feel important. When you commit to the betterment of all members of your team, no matter their role, they will buy into your cause, work autonomously and create priceless value for your customers.

Happy, loyal employees create happy, loyal customers. Their great customer service not only creates loyal customers, but it also brings in sales without spending more on advertising or marketing. Make every customer say WOW after they interact with your team by investing in your team's success with ongoing training and accountability, and you'll experience dividends from a healthy company culture.

Jump-Start Your Culture with Vision

To jump-start your company's culture, you need to create a vision—a living, breathing document that you use in your hiring, training, and even firing process. Your vision consists of your company's purpose, mission, and core values. Your *purpose* is like a guiding star that serves as your overarching aim. M*ission,* on the other hand, is a tangible goal, or set of goals, that can be accomplished in three years or less. *Core values* include a list of beliefs that you and your team share.

Every great company known for its customer service has a purpose, mission, and core values. If you do not have a vision, I strongly advise that you create one to support and direct your company culture. How? Get your vision about 75% complete and then present it to your team. Give them ownership of the vision and allow them to "take it home" and create the remaining 25%. I caution you to set aside ample time to create your vision. It took me three days with my team to complete the 25%, as well as one year of small tweaks to get it 100% right. Your vision, once created, will fuel and drive your company culture. Owners must commit to their vision for their teams to commit. After creating your vision, commit to it, 100%, so that it can be something that regularly inspires you and your team.

How to Create a WOW Culture

How do you teach this WOW mindset to individuals? How do you create a WOW culture? How do you get individuals and teams to stop seeing their work as a set of tasks and begin creating WOW Experiences that edify them and their clients? The foundation for such a change is a strong culture within your company, centered on creating that WOW.

To deliver products and services with a WOW Experience built into them, you must make the WOW Experience part of the product/service design, and that requires a culture that lives and breathes your company vision. *Vision* is not just a statement that hangs on the wall. You refer to it in every meeting and in every form of communication you send out to your team. It is your banner that you hold up for all to see and follow. It is **who** you are. When you see your company vision (if you have one), ask yourself, *"What are we doing to show that we believe in our vision?"*

Since WOW Experiences are unique gestures, they are not born out of rules or "best practices," but emerge as creative expressions of your company's culture—its shared values, and ideals. These values and ideals influence employees' decisions, thus creating exceptional outcomes. You can embed these culture factors into your products and services by always being aware of the long-term value of delivering a WOW Experience. The whole team must remain focused on living your vision daily, and being proactive in keeping it at the forefront of all activity. Otherwise, it can easily get derailed or forgotten. It is up to you as the leader to ensure your team understands and "buys into" the vision to establish a culture that consistently creates WOW.

Create a Vision Canvas

To enable you to adapt to changing scenarios, we recommend that you create and codify a *Vision Canvas* in your culture. Try these 10 practices:

1. Print your *Vision* onto a life-size canvas and glue or tape it to a rigid surface so that you can easily move it around.
2. Place the *Vision Canvas* where your team works, at project management sessions, in the break room, etc.
3. Use different colors of sticky notes for company ideas and innovations based on market changes to put on your *Vision Canvas* and to color-code different situations or opportunities.
4. Keep these sticky notes on the *Canvas* for reference in future work sessions.
5. When making product-market-fit decisions that respond to customer feedback or when considering the intended innovation of product/service features, ask whether the integrity of the company culture is preserved in these changes.
6. When facing a crisis, refer to the *Canvas*. In light of impending chaos or unexpected challenges, staying aligned with your vision is the best course of action.

7. When doing competitive analysis, assess how your vision improves your customer's WOW Experience.

8. When assessing your customer's WOW Experience, record the most meaningful stories and metrics that express your vision's impact.

9. When improving your product/service, assess what actions should be in place to enhance the culture.

10. When product/service performance decreases, determine whether all necessary core values are being expressed to sustain the customer's WOW Experience.

These are only a few tips to get you going with the *Vision Canvas*. When you hang your vision in a place of prominence, you will create a powerful WOW Culture in your company.

14 Sustaining WOW Performance

Start working now at an autonomous level

Pre-assessment question: What type of autonomy are you providing and supporting?

*A*utonomous work, coupled with a few key interpersonal skills, create a Pattern for Excellence in your relationships, your work and results. When you sustain WOW Performance, you'll have more freedom and become indispensable. You will experience fulfillment as you go above and beyond expected norms, both at work and home, by *giving first* to create WOW Experiences and creating unexpected value. When your performance creates WOW, you move people and change their disposition. You make them want to come back and have another great experience; and when you consistently deliver, people will likely tell all their friends about you.

Compelling examples of word-of-mouth marketing, exemplary leadership and teams working autonomously are: **Truett Cathy**, founder of Chick-Fil-A, one of the only fast food restaurants in America that closes on Sundays yet still brings in more money per location than McDonalds; **Steve Jobs** returning to Apple and creating a unique vision and customer experience; and **Walt Disney** with his supporting cast who create such magic. These visionary leaders produced well-documented success stories. They each had a cause so compelling that many people aligned with their cause and worked together at an autonomous level.

Working Autonomously to Create WOW

Performing at this level to create WOW Experiences for your clients, co-workers and family requires that you see meaning in your work and that it fulfills you

If I were to ask you to clean your room and add the restriction, "You can't go out and play until you do," you will likely approach this task as an obligation. You'll likely do the bare minimum. You'll throw all of your stuff underneath the bed or cram it in dresser drawers. You'll grab the top cover on your bed and throw it over the crumpled-up sheets underneath. You might sweep dirty socks under the bed or nightstands where others can't see. Why do we react this way? It is not about the responsibility—it is about getting the job done as quickly as possible so you can move on to something more meaningful, or fun.

The same storyline holds true at work. When you were hired to do your first job, you were likely more concerned about getting paid than about creating WOW experiences by doing exceptional work. For example, shortly after I was married, I laid cement for $12 an hour. I only lasted one month. Why? You couldn't pay me enough to wake up at four a.m. every morning to push cement back and forth. Moreover, many of my co-workers had addiction problems, been in jail, and used vulgar language. At first, I thought that I could work with them without becoming like them until one day I noticed the words coming out of *my* mouth. Why? When you subject yourself to any culture for ten hours a day, it begins to rub off on you, especially when you are young. I thought, "Man, no amount of money can motivate me to do this work every day."

What if the circumstances, culture or purpose of the cement work changed? Imagine my boss sharing that we were hired to lay cement pro bono to form the foundation of a school for kids with special needs. This non-profit organization had to move into a larger building because they had outgrown their space and had nowhere to put all the kids in need. Wouldn't this change the picture? All of a sudden the motivation changes. Why? Because the purpose of the work changed; it became larger than me. Now it was more important than the money, how hard the work was or how long it took.

Sustaining WOW Performance requires you to excel in five things:

1) Create a worthy cause and hire good people who believe in it
2) Give them responsibilities or specific roles to play and create value in your cause
3) Provide a way to track and report their progress
4) Believe that together you can do and create amazing things
5) Empower; invite active engagement with clients and fellow team members, and continually reinforce the collective cause to motivate and embolden them in their work.

Ultimately, the Pattern for Excellence puts you and your team in a strong emotional state, coupled with mastery of interpersonal skills where you can collectively do your best work. In this *culture of caring*, this *environment of empowerment*, all stakeholders receive as much personal fulfillment, if not more, in the pursuit of the cause than in its attainment. You come to love the process, not just the finished product. You enjoy your work more and do it better. You perform at a much higher level because the work has great meaning.

Autonomous work is about freedom. It is about going above and beyond the call of duty, independently and interdependently. It is about being self-driven in your responsibilities in pursuit of a purpose.

WOW Performance happens when your actions are aligned with your values. The resulting association makes you feel good as you do your work. When guided by principles, you experience an inner drive to perform your best work—not because you are told to, but because the work fulfills you. It makes you happy.

You are *motivated* to do the work with or without an audience; with or without supervision. You perform at a high level regardless of whether you like the hours or the pay because of the way you feel when you do the work. This shift in thinking comes because you stop seeing the work as menial tasks and begin to see a bigger picture and your part in it. As long as the vision, or cause within that vision, is something you are passionate about, you will see the value in the work and will be motivated to go above and beyond what is expected.

What's the key to Self-Motivation?

Can self-motivation be found in a certain mandate, system or script?

Mandate. Since providing exceptional service is necessary to stay in business, you may require (mandate) your employees to provide excellent customer service; however, you'll soon find that they see it as one more task to be completed; another obligation. In the end, you can't force or mandate people to provide excellent service.

System. You can no longer afford to have your team merely go through the motions or do the minimum work necessary by following your system, process, policy or procedural checklist.

Script. Canned scripts do not accommodate the various types of customers you encounter or the disposition in which you find them. Also, call handling teams in all industries often fear autonomous work because they think they are supposed to follow the script.

I conclude: *No mandate, system or script—no matter how well intended and thought out—will guarantee consistent value creation*. The service your CSRs provide customers has to be awesome, and *awesome service springs from self-motivation*!

You must find and develop people who are *motivated* by your vision to provide great service and help others see the *joy* of creating amazing service experiences. Your team likely already knows what *great service* looks and feels like, but for some reason, they are not able or choose not to provide it. What's holding them back? Perhaps they feel things aren't going the way they should in your company or that they're not getting along with their co-workers. They may not like you. They may not like your customers. They may not like their job, or are not passionate about it.

The Pattern for Excellence enables you to provide the training and positive motivation your team needs to deliver phenomenal service *of their own volition* (self-motivation). They'll provide great service with a different *motive*—without consideration for a raise in income, new regulation, or for social recognition. They'll provide great service because they want to—not because they are told or mandated.

New Science of Motivation: Autonomy, Mastery, and Purpose

People believe that the best way to motivate is to use tangible incentives like money, recognition, and rewards. However, Daniel Pink, author of the provocative and persuasive book *Drive: The Surprising Truth About What Motivates Us*, suggests that the secret to high performance and satisfaction consists of three human needs or *three pillars*:

1) To direct our own lives (autonomy)
2) To become better at things that matter to us (mastery)
3) To do something meaningful for ourselves and the world (purpose).

Pink argues that people are *purpose maximizers* and suggests that managers and leaders should implement a new way of motivating people based on the three pillars.

Autonomy—the desire to direct our lives. Pink states that, *"People need autonomy over task (what they do), time (when they do it), team (who they do it with), and technique (how they do it)."* Practice born of principle and purpose creates autonomous work.

> *Autonomy* is the freedom from external control or influence; independence.
>
> —*Google Free Dictionary*

How can we deliver phenomenal WOW service consistently? We first seek to help our employees and associates in the pursuit of happiness to perform autonomous work. It is in turning outward that we begin to create consistent WOW service.

The principle of *autonomy* had a big impact on me. I heard a young retired Navy Seal use the word a year ago, and I was fascinated by it and researched its meaning. Autonomy occurs when your actions and values are aligned to achieve a predetermined outcome of extreme importance. People are happiest and do their best work when they are engaged in a cause far greater than themselves; when they forget themselves and go to work. Look at The Revolutionary War. American patriots were outmanned and outgunned, but the cause was clear. From their experience, learning and faith, our founding fathers developed a superior form of government that ensured the rights and freedoms of its citizens. The cause was greater than themselves, and they were willing to give their lives for it. No one was mandating or motivating them to place their lives on the line.

Control leads to compliance; autonomy leads to engagement. *Autonomy* implies that people have some degree of control over their work. *Autonomous behavior* means that people act with a sense of volition and choice. It promotes greater conceptual understanding, better grades, enhanced persistence at school and in sporting activities, higher productivity, less burnout, and greater psychological well-being. Autonomy is different from independence because autonomy gives people the opportunity to act with choice.

One way to establish autonomy in the workforce is to create a results-oriented workplace where people don't have schedules— they show up when they want and don't have to be in the office at a particular time. The only requirement is that they get their work done and show their results. Autonomy emerges when people have a choice over their tasks, time, technique, and team. Autonomy stimulates intrinsic motivation, and people with high intrinsic motivation are usually better coworkers.

Mastery—the urge to become better at something that matters. Mastery means that people want to get better at what they do. Mastery requires engagement and begins with flow—optimal experiences when the challenges you face are exquisitely matched to your abilities. Mastery of the mechanics behind what you do makes you equal to the opportunity before you. Keep in mind that opportunity is all around us. Pink suggests that smart workplaces supplement day-to-day activities with *Goldilocks tasks*—not too hard and not too easy. There are four rules of mastery:

1) Mastery is a mindset that requires the capacity to see your abilities not as finite, but as infinitely improvable
2) Mastery is demanding; it requires effort, grit and deliberate practice
3) Mastery is an asymptote that is impossible to realize fully, meaning there is always room for improvement
4) Mastery of the principles of the Pattern for Excellence is a journey, not a destination.

Purpose—the yearning to be part of something larger than ourselves. We all want to be part of something that is bigger than we are. The goal is to maximize purpose, not monthly numbers. So, how can we take these principles and engage people? It's difficult to get to a spot where it feels okay to think outside the box; however, when you grant the permission to think freely, solutions suddenly surface organically.

Your purpose is the anticipated outcome or reason why you choose your guiding principles and practices. When your behavior and actions have a purpose, you work with an intended outcome in mind. Purpose gives way to focus, determination, and the passion to achieve your end goal—independent of circumstances or outside forces.

When your time is devoted to a cause greater than self, you lose track of time. Fears are set aside. Technique and stamina are enhanced. Old habitual distractions dissipate and begin to lose their grip. All that matters is the progress and success you experience in doing the work. Viktor Frankl noted that the search for meaning is the basic motivation of human life. We are not in pursuit of happiness; instead, we search for reasons to be happy.

Unfortunately, most companies focus on *profit maximization* rather than *purpose maximization*. Purpose is a nice thing to have as long as it does not get in the way of making a profit for the company. However, the best companies focus on maximizing their profit by maximizing their purpose. These companies usually express purpose based motives in the goals they set. Goals that use profit to reach purpose deemphasizing self-interest and upholding policies that allow people to pursue purpose on their own terms.

Apple is a company that is focused on maximizing their profit by maximizing their purpose. Apple's primary goal is to create great products that everyone can enjoy. They seek to make life easier for people, and they achieve this through technology. By maximizing their purpose, Apple is maximizing its profit because people love their products.

What is Motivation?

The word *motivation* comes from the Latin verb *movere*, which means *to move*. Motivation makes us move from point A to point B. Ever heard of *carrots and sticks*? The principle of *carrots and sticks* is a motivation system based on *rewards and punishment*. Many organizations still use this principle to motivate their employees and increase productivity. However, Daniel Pink suggests that when it comes to motivation, there is a gap between what science knows and what business does. The current operating system for most businesses is built around external, carrot-and-stick motivators, which often backfires.

Evolution of Motivation

Here's a very brief history of the evolution of motivation:

Motivation 1.0: hunger, thirst, shelter, and reproduction. Think of people living in caves.

Motivation 2.0: rewards and punishment to manipulate behavior—if you do this, you will get that—a carrot-and-stick approach that influences peoples' behavior using external rewards.

Motivation 3.0: the three elements of true motivation are autonomy, mastery, and purpose. People will be most creative when they feel motivated primarily by personal interest, enjoyment, satisfaction, and the challenge of the work itself rather than by external pressures.

What's wrong with extrinsic motivation? Extrinsic motivation is based on the idea that if we want to produce a certain behavior we need to reward it; and if we don't want that behavior, we must repress it using punishment. However, when people are motivated by external rewards, they shift their attention from the experience leading to the goal, to the reward that follows the goal. Pure focus on goals may cause systematic problems, such as focusing only on short-term gains and losing sight of the potentially devastating long-term effects on the organization.

The symptoms of a goals-only focus include: Narrowed focus, unethical behavior, increased risk-taking, decreased cooperation, and decreased intrinsic motivation.

This does not mean that everyone should stop using external rewards. Rather, for routine tasks—ones that are not very interesting and don't require creative thinking—rewards can provide a small motivational booster shot without harmful side effects.

> *"You have to build up each player to be his best as a guard, center, or forward, but it is even more important to develop the individual player's pride and belief in the whole team and its goals."*
>
> —John Wooden,
> *former basketball coach of the UCLA Bruins*

Born to Create

At the start of this book, I mentioned that the autism of my youngest son, Hagen, was the main catalyst for getting me into the customer service coaching and training business. My wife and I toyed with several ideas back in 2008. I couldn't find a job that would provide enough for the family plus Hagen's therapy. The path was clear—we needed to start another business. We considered everything from frozen yogurt to a bread shop. At the end of the day, however, I knew that if I was not passionate about what I was doing, there was no chance of long-term success.

I worked hard, gave first and soon found an opportunity to start a business quite by accident. It was an industry I had worked in for years. I could speak the industry's language, use the contacts I had already developed, and provide the best solution to a common problem (poor customer service and lost sales).

At the time, an email that I received as I was boarding a flight made all the difference. The email came from a talented therapist who worked with my son. Hagen was five years and could not speak a word. He only mimicked us when we spoke or used sign language first. Hagen is a very athletic boy—a flight risk who does not know to stop for traffic. We have three locks on each door that lead outside so we can keep him indoors. He is fast, agile, and often outruns me (and I can run a six-minute mile). Hopefully, he runs towards the park as opposed to the road. The moment I look away is the moment he goes. He is smart but his autism causes a lack of judgment. The backstory of the email is what makes it so special.

There was a link in the email to a video of Hagen. It began with the therapist asking Hagen, "What's your name?" I sat there on the plane moments before it took off, watching a miracle on my iPad. I played it over and over again, watching my son say his name for the first time. Tears streamed down my face as I continued to watch the short 10 seconds of video until the cell phone reception ended at 10,000 feet. I folded my arms and prayed silently, thanking God for what I had just seen. I was on my way to speak in Cincinnati, Ohio. I did not think to change my presentation until I saw the video of my son. I couldn't imagine anything more important than what I had just seen, so I started writing a new presentation.

My objective was simple: To thank everyone, express my gratitude for having the opportunity to serve them which enabled me to support my family and help my son. Flying at 30,000 feet, I asked myself, "What motivates people? What gets them to do their best work? Is it money or recognition? No, it's a good cause—one that is bigger than them."

My wife is constantly working on fundraisers for kids with autism. Although she would not have chosen this cause if not for Hagen, I have never met anyone more talented or more courageous in my life. She has raised hundreds of thousands of dollars without receiving one penny in return. Why? She cannot think of anything worse than a parent who does not have the money or the support necessary to give their child with autism, or any special need for that matter, the help that they need. "This is my last fundraiser" she always says. I don't believe it for a moment. During each event, she says the same thing, but when it's over, she begins to work on the next one. She puts 100% into every fundraiser, and then looks back and wishes she had done more. She's an incredible person. It is the cause that motivates her work. You see, it is bigger than her...it is bigger than me.

The author of the *E-Myth*, Michael Gerber, states, "If we are born in the image of God, and I believe that we are, then we are born to create." When I heard my son utter his name for the first time, I remembered my *Why*. When I learned that my son had autism and what it would cost to help him, I began to create. I would not be capable of doing what I do today unless I had a huge *Why*. Learning our son had autism—that our son needed therapy to have a chance at a normal life gave me my *Why*. I was motivated like never before to create the means to provide for him and the rest of our family. When I walked in to speak with the first group of therapists about my son, I was broke and unsure what I should do. I walked out motivated to create, because I had no other choice. There was no other way. I had to find a problem I could solve better than anyone else. My wife also began to create in her own way, giving of her time and energy to help others.

In Cincinnati, Ohio, the audience I was training learned what a good cause looks like when they saw my son say his name for the first time—a cause that was bigger than them and a cause that was bigger than me. And I knew that if I could help them get what they wanted, they would help me get what I needed. I'll never forget the experience I had that day, and I cannot thank the industry enough for the opportunity afforded me.

In a WOW Experience, the Giver freely provides an amazing service that the Receiver did not expect. Both are edified because the Receiver is visibly impressed by the service provided. When Givers witness the Receiver's gratefulness, the Givers feel so good that they are self-motivated to provide the same kind of service over and over again. All doubt and questioning of the purpose and vision are set aside because they feel the remarkable joy of serving others.

When you find purpose in your work, you will unlock a latent ability to create WOW Experiences for others. The more WOW Experiences you create, the more Receivers will benefit—and the more fulfilled your life will become. Remember, you are born to create.

> *"People will be self-motivated when doing work they believe in. A guiding aim, when clear and shared, is so powerful that it can even form the backbone of motivation for an entire country."*
>
> —Jim Collins and Bill Lazier,
> *Beyond Entrepreneurship*

Refine Your Vision: Values, Mission & Purpose

As a final petition, I encourage you to refine your vision, consisting of core values, mission, and purpose (based on the Collins-Porras *Vision Framework*):

Core values: A system of guiding principles; a philosophy of business and life.

- Principles that are to be held inviolate
- An extension of the personal core values and beliefs of the leader(s)
- Changes to core values rarely happen, if ever

Mission: a bold, compelling audacious goal.

- Has a clear finish line and a specific time-frame, and once completed, a new mission is set

- Changes whenever one mission is completed, and a new one needs to be set (usually every five to 15 years)

Purpose: The fundamental reason for the organization's existence.

- Grows out of Core Values
- Like a guiding star: always worked towards but never fully attained
- Should serve to guide the company for 100 years

Timeless Truth ala Zig Ziglar

Both Alexander the Great and Cortez could motivate others to work on their cause or die trying. I was extremely motivated by my son's needs and knew I had to do something on my own. I had to help enough people get what they wanted so they could help me with what I needed. I listened to and read several motivational books and CDs. I wrote and recorded my thoughts and impressions. I was driven like never before.

During that time, I was privileged to experience one of Zig Ziglar's last speeches. When Zig came to Salt Lake City, Utah, my college friend had an extra ticket. I was very excited to hear him speak, even though he had been having trouble giving his speeches lately. In fact, Zig's daughter had to be on stage with him to cue him on each segment. He had lost his short-term memory because of a recent fall in his home, but he did not disappoint.

> *"You can get everything in life you want if you will just help enough other people get what they want."*
>
> —Zig Ziglar

There was a moment in Zig's speech when I sensed that he spoke just to me, even though there were 20,000 people in the Vivint

Arena. Zig said that he met a preacher in his youth who was so good at encouraging others that he knew that was exactly what he wanted to do. He continued encouraging others, well into his 80's.

It was then that I realized what I was meant to do. I wanted to teach and to serve. At the time, I didn't know exactly what I would say or do to encourage others, but I knew that as I persisted, the words, phrases, principles and purpose would come. Aristotle said, "We are what we repeatedly do. Excellence then is not an act, but a habit." The Pattern for Excellence came to me over time as I endeavored to teach and encourage others. I don't claim that the principles are original—there are many books on positivity, confidence, listening, and all the rest. The difference, however, is in the sequence and power of the Master Principles.

It is not enough to know the principles—you must experience them and master them.

> *"Life battles don't always go to the stronger or faster man. Sooner or later the man who wins is the man who thinks he can."*
>
> —coach Vince Lombardi.

I am definitely not the smartest or the fastest guy. My son needed a chance at a normal life, and I was out of options. I was motivated to find a problem and solve it. I endeavored with all my might to solve it. As I applied the principles I was learning in my studies; I taught others. When my clients applied these principles, they experienced success and fulfillment in their work. As they experienced true joy and success, so did I. WOW Experiences multiplied.

People Want to Be Self-Directed

Once people are paid enough to get the question of money off the table, give them a chance to look beyond reward-based, extrinsic motivation. People want to be self-directed; they like to master things, and they want to be a part of something important. If we start treating people like they are worthy and valuable, not to be manipulated by rewards and punishment, we can improve work engagement, increase happiness, and make the world a better place.

Once customers learn that you routinely provide awesome service, they become more tolerant even when they buy your product or use your service and have an experience that's not so impressive. Imagine what it would be like to have clients who are tolerant, even when you mess up every once in a while! Your loyal clients like you because of the WOW Experiences you create and will come back as long as you continue to go out of your way to serve them.

The Pattern for Excellence is about doing meaningful work that fulfills you. A WOW Experience is that moment when your client recognizes that you went above and beyond. Expressions such as "WOW" are often used by clients to describe how you created value for them in an unexpected way and won the moment—this is WOW Performance…autonomy in action.

In the end, the Pattern for Excellence frees us from circumstances and mental blocks to communicate effectively with others in the pursuit of meaning. So…get going! Apply the Eight Master Principles in the Pattern for Excellence to create WOW for others intentionally, time and time again.

ENDNOTES

1. http://renewyourmind.co.nz/retrain-brain-neuroplasticity-in-action/ The Brain by chantal
2 http://science.howstuffworks.com/innovation/everyday-innovations/how-to-make-potato-powered-light-bulb.htm (accessed August 2016)
3 http://www.skininc.com/skinscience/physiology/17969919.html#sthash.hf0iJQH9.dpuf (Accessed August 2016)
4 http://www.theatlantic.com/health/archive/2012/04/how-the-power-of-positive-thinking-won-scientific-credibility/256223/) (Accessed July 2016)

ABOUT THE AUTHOR AND COMPANY

Brigham Dickinson is president and founder of Power Selling Pros, a leading coaching training firm dedicated to teaching call handling teams to wow more customers. Their goal is to solve problems for companies entrenched in the service industry and help their businesses grow. In 2009 Brigham's company trained 6 call handlers, now the team trains over 450 in 130 companies worldwide.

Growth is fueled primarily by referrals, thanks to their proven call-handling certification process and high customer satisfaction. Brigham initially created the Pattern for Excellence for call handling teams. The sequence of principles guides call handlers through greeting, rapport development, reassurance, building confidence, booking the appointment and call closure. Since then the Pattern for Excellence has evolved into a powerful sales tool where anyone can create WOW Experiences for their customers, regardless of their position in their organization.

Brigham developed a powerful solution through Customer Service Representative (CSR) and Dispatcher (DSR) training and coaching. Consumer feedback toward local business, whether good or bad, is now being shared, in real time, on popular search and social media platforms. This feedback plays an important role in steering a consumer's perception of your business. The call handling team interacts with the people who write and post this real-time feedback. With regular training, call handling teams will deliver a powerfully positive service experience to consumers, and influence the way people view your company.

Brigham hires good people who forget themselves in the work, gives them a few specific roles to play in the cause, gives them a way to track and report on their progress, and believes that they will create amazing things. He empowers them to fulfill their responsibilities in their own way, provides empowerment, invites their continual engagement among clients and fellow team members and reinforces the collective cause to motivate and embolden them.

If you hope to set your company apart from the competition in a commoditized market, we can help. We will listen to at least 100 of your phone calls and pinpoint specific steps you can take to WOW more customers. When you create more WOW experiences, you'll book more calls and make more money. This free service includes a report and consultation from a Certified Call Handling Trainer. Call us and ask for a free report and consultation today. We offer a proven training system that helps your Call Handling Team create Wow Experiences over the phone. Your CSRs will book at least two additional calls per day—that's a quarter of a million dollars in extra revenue a year—without adding expense to your marketing or advertising budget.

Contact Brigham's team today! Email us at info@powersellingpros.com or call us at (801) 253-1004 to learn how we can help your service team to book more calls, WOW more customers and make more money! Or, email Brigham directly: brigham@powersellingpros.com or Visit www.powersellingpros.com